Study 1

Dispensational Truth

Study to shew thyself approved unto God, a workman that needeth not to be ashamed, rightly dividing the word of truth. (2 Tim. 2:15)

David O'Steen

All Rights Reserved

No part of this book may be reproduced, or stored in a retrieval system, or transmitted in any form or by any means, electronic, mechanical, photocopying, recording, or otherwise, without express written permission of the publisher.

First Printed in April 2020
Second Edition December 2022

Library of Congress Control Number: 2018675309
Printed in the United States of America

The Study Notes Series

The *skeleton* of information in the Study Notes Series was compiled from my personal Bible study notes. I have worked to *put some meat on the bones* in an effort to make the notes more readable for others. These books are not wordy commentaries, but they are more than just a collection of outlines.

This book is designed to function as a study guide and companion to our video series on Right Division (go to hopebiblechurchga.com and click on Video under Resources).

I do not claim complete originality for every thought and outline found within this book. I am thankful for the help that I have gleaned from other dispensational Bible teachers.

All scripture references are taken from the Authorized King James Bible (except those used to show corruption in the modern versions).

The final authority is the word of God (2 Tim. 3:16). Please take the time to search the scriptures and see whether these things are so (Acts 17:11; 1 Thess. 5:21).

It is my heart's desire and prayer that God will use this book for His glory and the edification of the saints.

David O'Steen
Jackson, Georgia

Table of Contents

Introduction 5
1. Privilege and Responsibility 7
2. Motives Matter in Bible Study 10
3. The Word of Truth 15
4. Nine Rules for Fruitful Bible Study 26
5. The Basics of Dispensational Truth 30
6. The Apostle Paul 40
7. Mysteries in the Bible 53
8. The Main Division 61
9. The Twofold Purpose of God 67
10. The Twofold Ministry of Christ 74
11. The Twofold People of God 76
12. The Book Between 86
13. Things That Differ 91
14. More Things That Differ 105
15. Dispensational Salvation 122
16. What About Signs? 129
17. A Word of Caution 132
18. Defending Dispensational Truth 143
19. The Necessity of Rightly Dividing 150
20. The Fight is On 155

Introduction

...Understandest thou what thou readest? (Acts 8:30b)

That was the question Phillip asked the Ethiopian eunuch as he sat in his chariot reading the book of Isaiah. The eunuch responded, "How can I, except some man should guide me?" He did not know if the prophecy in Isaiah 53 was about the prophet himself or some other man. He did not have the spiritual understanding to see it was about Christ because he was yet to receive the Holy Spirit. He needed a spiritual man to show him Christ in the scriptures.

There are many people who read the Bible but do not understand it. How important is it that we have understanding? It is a "wellspring of life unto him that hath it" (Prov. 16:22). We cannot "walk worthy of the Lord unto all pleasing, being fruitful in every good work, and increasing in the knowledge of God" without "spiritual understanding" (Col. 1:9-10).

Spiritual understanding comes from receiving the spiritual light of God's word.

The entrance of thy words giveth <u>light</u>; it giveth <u>understanding</u> unto the simple. (Ps. 119:130)

We need the Spirit of God to illuminate our understanding to the spiritual truth of the scripture. We cannot know the spiritual things of God without the Spirit of God (1 Cor. 2:9-12). The Lord must open our understanding to His truth (Lk. 24:45).

The Spirit of God dwells in every believer (Rom. 8:9). We are brought out of darkness into God's light the moment we believe the gospel (Acts 26:18; Eph. 5:8). Sadly, most people are blinded to the gospel of the grace of God because they have only heard counterfeit gospels (2 Cor. 4:3-4; 11:4) that pervert the message by adding works (Gal. 1:6-12). They must hear the gospel light that Christ died for our sins, was buried, and rose again the third day (1 Cor. 15:3-4). We are saved by grace the moment we believe the gospel of Christ (Rom. 1:16; Eph. 1:13).

Salvation is instantaneous, but spiritual growth is a process. Therefore, saved people can still be in darkness to certain spiritual truths. The religious traditions of men blind people to the truth of God's word. For example, the apostle Paul prayed for believers to have the eyes of their understanding enlightened that they might know "what is the hope of his calling" (Eph. 1:18). Sadly, the majority of professing Christians today do not know the truth about our blessed hope (Titus 2:13).

The Spirit of God will enable us to understand the word of God as we sincerely believe it and study it His way (2 Tim. 2:15). We must depend upon the Spirit of God if we are going to be serious students of the scripture. As we believe and walk in the light that He gives us, He will give us more and more light (Prov. 4:18).

We must study the Bible in light of where we are living in God's plan of the ages. Christ raised up the apostle Paul to be the pattern and spokesman to the Body of Christ in this present age of grace. That is why he said,

Consider what I say; and the Lord give thee understanding in all things. (2 Tim. 2:7)

Chapter 1
Privilege and Responsibility

What a great blessing and privilege it is to have the inspired word of God preserved in our own language! The King James Bible has proven itself to be the pure word of God for over four hundred years. With great privilege comes great responsibility.

Here are seven things that we should do with our Bible every day.

1) **Read** – Simply reading the Bible is where we must begin.

Seek ye out of the book of the LORD, and read: (Isa. 34:16a)

Till I come, give attendance to reading, to exhortation, to doctrine. (1 Tim. 4:13)

2) **Study** – Studying the Bible is more intense than reading it. We must examine it carefully with the purpose of understanding what it says.

Study to shew thyself approved unto God, a workman that needeth not to be ashamed, rightly dividing the word of truth. (2 Tim. 2:15)

3) **Meditate** – To meditate on the word of God is to think deeply upon the truth we have learned through personal Bible study. We will not be "nourished up in the words of

faith and of good doctrine" (1 Tim. 4:6) without meditating on what we are learning as we study God's word. Meditation is to the spirit what digestion is to the body.

Meditate upon these things; give thyself wholly to them; that thy profiting may appear to all. (1 Tim. 4:15)

4) **Hide it in our heart** – As we meditate on the truth, it will dwell in our heart.

Thy word have I hid in mine heart, that I might not sin against thee. (Ps. 119:11)

Let the word of Christ dwell in you richly in all wisdom; teaching and admonishing one another in psalms and hymns and spiritual songs, singing with grace in your hearts to the Lord. (Col. 3:16)

5) **Apply** – Learning the Bible should have a personal impact on our lives.

(6) If thou put the brethren in remembrance of these things, thou shalt be a good minister of Jesus Christ, nourished up in the words of faith and of good doctrine, whereunto thou hast attained.
(7) But refuse profane and old wives' fables, and exercise thyself rather unto godliness. (1 Tim. 4:6-7)

6) **Obey** – There is doctrine in the Bible that we must not only learn, but also obey.

But God be thanked, that ye were the servants of sin, but ye have obeyed from the heart that form of doctrine which was delivered you. (Rom. 6:17)

> 7) **Teach** – We must pass on the truth we have learned to others. If we cannot communicate what we have learned, we have not truly learned it.

And the things that thou hast heard of me among many witnesses, the same commit thou to faithful men, who shall be able to teach others also. (2 Tim. 2:2)

Chapter 2
Motives Matter in Bible Study

Bible study should not be about just gaining knowledge, but about growing in our spiritual knowledge of God. We know God and His truth through His word, not through our own thoughts, feelings, or experiences. Therefore, our Bible study should be a spiritual exercise and not an academic one because the Bible is the living word of God and not a theological textbook.

Why did the apostle Paul say that we must study to be "approved unto God" (2 Tim. 2:15)? Are we not complete in Christ (Col. 2:10) and accepted in Him (Eph. 1:6) the moment we believe the gospel? We are approved as to our **standing** (i.e., our unchangeable position in Christ), but he is talking about our **state** (i.e., our changeable condition in this life).

We must all stand before the judgment seat of Christ to give an account of our service (Rom. 14:10-19; 1 Cor. 4:1-5; 2 Cor. 5:9-11). We will not know how to serve God according to His will unless we rightly divide the word of truth and follow Paul, the "wise masterbuilder" whom God used to lay the foundation for this present age, which is Jesus Christ "according to the revelation of the mystery" (Rom. 16:25).

(10) According to the grace of God which is given unto me, as a wise masterbuilder, I have laid the foundation, and another buildeth thereon. But let every man take heed how he buildeth thereupon.

(11) For other foundation can no man lay than that is laid, which is Jesus Christ.
(12) Now if any man build upon this foundation gold, silver, precious stones, wood, hay, stubble;
(13) Every man's work shall be made manifest: for the day shall declare it, because it shall be revealed by fire; and the fire shall try every man's work of what sort it is.
(14) If any man's work abide which he hath built thereupon, he shall receive a reward.
(15) If any man's work shall be burned, he shall suffer loss: but he himself shall be saved; yet so as by fire.
(1 Cor. 3:10-15)

What are our motives in Bible study?
1) The fear of God (Prov. 1:7), or man (Prov. 29:25)?
2) The approval of God (2 Tim. 2:15), or man (Jn. 12:42-43)?
3) The judgment seat of Christ, or the judgment of men (1 Cor. 4:1-5)?
4) Charity (1 Cor. 13:2), or pride (1 Cor. 8:1)?

Does our Bible study cause us to grow spiritually (2 Tim. 3:17)? Do we study that we might minister to others, or look down on them? God knows our heart, and motives matter in how we serve Him (1 Cor. 4:5).

The Bible is made up of spiritual words that are spiritually discerned. We must rely upon the Spirit of God, who inspired the scripture, to illuminate our hearts and minds to its spiritual truth (1 Cor. 2:6-16).

A person cannot understand the spiritual truth of the Bible unless they are saved.

Are You Saved?

Before we go any further, please stop and sincerely consider the most important question.

This question should receive a "Yes" or "No" answer, but it almost never does. Some of the most common responses are:
- I'm doing the best I can.
- I prayed the sinner's prayer.
- I've made Jesus the Lord of my life.
- I believe in God.
- I've been baptized.
- I'm a church member.
- I keep the commandments.
- I am basically a good person.
- I walked the aisle and prayed through.
- I've always been a Christian.
- I've never done anything really bad.

None of these responses properly answer the question. People give these kinds of responses because they evidently do not understand the question. The question, "Are you saved?" asks whether or not you have trusted Christ's shed blood on the cross as payment for your sins. It is not asking about any works that you can do. The responses listed above refer to what a person does, but salvation is only offered on the basis of what Christ has already done for us.

The gospel of our salvation (Eph. 1:13) is clearly stated by the apostle Paul in the following passage.

(3) For I delivered unto you first of all that which I also received, how that Christ died for our sins according to the scriptures;
(4) And that he was buried, and that he rose again the third day according to the scriptures. (1 Cor. 15:3-4)

The blood of Christ has purchased what we could not earn ourselves.

In whom we have redemption through his blood, even the forgiveness of sins: (Col. 1:14)

We cannot be good enough to earn salvation because **"there is none righteous"** (Rom. 3:10) and **"all have sinned"** (Rom. 3:23). The **"wages of sin is death"** (Rom. 6:23). Those who die lost will spend eternity in **"the lake of fire"** (Rev. 20:15).

In order to be saved, we must stop trusting ourselves and trust the blood payment that Christ has already made on our behalf!

(8) For by grace are ye saved through faith; and that not of yourselves: it is the gift of God:
(9) Not of works, lest any man should boast. (Eph. 2:8-9)

Jesus Christ fully accomplished our salvation through His death, burial, and resurrection. Therefore, the free gift of salvation can only be received by faith alone in His finished work.

Therefore being justified by faith, we have peace with God through our Lord Jesus Christ: (Rom. 5:1)

If you will trust Jesus Christ as your Saviour, you can enjoy **"much assurance"** (1 Thess. 1:5) that you are saved and on your way to heaven.

Chapter 3
The Word of Truth

The "word of truth" refers to both the gospel in particular (Eph. 1:13) and the word of God in general (Ps. 119:43). How could we know for sure that the gospel is true if the whole Bible is not true?

Believing the Bible (2 Tim. 3:16) and rightly dividing it (2 Tim. 2:15) go hand in hand. The only way to understand the Bible without changing any words is to rightly divide it. We must change our understanding to line up with the Bible, and never change the Bible to make it line up with our understanding.

The King James Bible (KJB) is a dispensational book, which is amazing in light of the fact that the translators were not dispensationalists.

- It is the only English translation that preserves the key to Bible study in 2 Timothy 2:15.
- It is also the only one that preserves Paul's doctrine of justification by the "faith of Christ."
- Its sixty-six books are laid out in dispensational order.
- It has a built-in dictionary and cross-referencing system that greatly helps us in rightly dividing the word of truth.

If we are going to study the Bible, we must be confident that the Bible we are studying is indeed the very words of God. Otherwise, what is the point? Our God is a God of absolute truth

(Jn. 14:6). Therefore, His word must be the truth (Jn. 17:17). The scripture gives many of the same titles, attributes, and works of the Lord Jesus Christ to itself. Therefore, to attack one is to attack the other, and to exalt one is to exalt the other.

Titles

"his name is called THE WORD OF GOD" (Rev. 19:13)
"sword of the Spirit, which is THE WORD OF GOD" (Eph. 6:17)

"the WORD OF LIFE" (1 Jn. 1:1)
"Holding forth the WORD OF LIFE" (Phil. 2:16)

Attributes

"I am... the TRUTH" (Jn. 14:6)
"the scripture of TRUTH" (Dan. 10:21)

"called FAITHFUL and TRUE" (Rev. 19:11)
"these words are TRUE and FAITHFUL" (Rev. 21:5)

"I am the LIGHT of the world" (Jn. 8:12)
"thy word... LIGHT" (Ps. 119:105)

"the Lord shall ENDURE for ever" (Ps. 9:7)
"the word of the Lord ENDURETH for ever" (1 Pet. 1:25)

Works

"BORN of God" (1 Jn. 5:4)
"BORN...by the word of God" (1 Pet. 1:23)

"the Son QUICKENETH whom He will" (Jn. 5:21)
"thy word hath QUICKENED me" (Ps. 119:50)

"Christ hath made us FREE" (Gal. 5:1)
"the truth shall make you FREE" (Jn. 8:32)

"out of his mouth goeth a sharp SWORD" (Rev. 19:15)
"word of God... sharper than any twoedged SWORD" (Heb. 4:12)

How We Should Respond

"Have FAITH in God" (Mk. 11:22)
"FAITH cometh... by the word of God" (Rom. 10:17)

"ye have therefore RECEIVED Christ Jesus the Lord" (Col. 2:6)
"ye RECEIVED the word of God" (1 Thess. 2:13)

"He that glorieth, let him GLORY in the Lord" (1 Cor. 1:31)
"the word of the Lord... be GLORIFIED" (2 Thess. 3:1)

The Infallible Word

Jesus Christ is called the "Word" because He reveals and declares the Father (Jn. 1:1, 14, 18). The Spirit inspired the word of God to reveal and declare Christ. There is an inseparable bond between the incarnate Word and the inspired word. One is God manifest in the flesh (1 Tim. 3:16), and the other is God manifest in a Book (2 Tim. 3:16). If Christ would have sinned just one time, He could not be "the Word of God" (Rev. 19:13). A Bible that has errors in it cannot be rightly called, "the word of truth" or "the word of God."

All three members of the Godhead are equally God, but the Son was sent to glorify the Father and the Spirit was sent to glorify the Son (Jn. 7:14-18; 16:12-15). The Holy Spirit, who inspired the scripture, glorifies the Son of God who is central in all the scripture (Jn. 5:39; 15:26). Therefore, any religious group that denies the deity of Christ or diminishes Him in any way is not of God, and any "Bible" that does the same is also not of God. The King James Bible honors and glorifies the Son of God more than all the modern English translations.

All the modern versions of the Bible diminish the person and work of Christ to some degree. Those who defend the modern versions might say, "But they don't do that in every passage!" Why would it be right or acceptable to do that even once? Some versions are worse than others, but just one error is serious! What if Christ had sinned just one time? This issue alone ought to be sufficient for any sincere Christian to reject the modern versions, not to mention the issues concerning the corrupt men, manuscripts, and methods behind them.

The spirit of Satan is at work in this world, especially in religion (Eph. 2:2; 2 Thess. 2:7). His great ambition is to be worshipped (Matt. 4:8-10). He is envious of the true Christ. Did you know that the NIV calls Satan and Christ by the same name ("morning star," Isa. 14:12; Rev. 22:16)? That's blasphemy! Satan has been producing new versions with doctrinal corruption. He is all about attacking the word of God (Gen. 3:1). He even had the audacity to tamper with the word of God when he was tempting the Word of God, Jesus Christ (Matt. 4:1-11). THE ISSUE in these last days is inspiration of scripture (2 Tim. 3:13-17).

Please consider the following comparison of the KJB (**bold**) with some of the modern versions (*italics*). More examples are given in Study Notes on the King James Bible by the same author.

The Deity of Christ

Mic. 5:2 But thou Bethlehem... out of thee shall he come forth unto me that is to be ruler in Israel; whose goings forth have been from of old, from <u>everlasting</u>. – *"whose origin is from of old, from ancient days" (RSV), "whose origins are from of old, from ancient times" (NIV), "whose coming forth is from of old, from ancient days" (ESV)*

Matt. 20:20 Then came to him the mother of Zebedee's children with her sons, <u>worshipping him</u>... – *"kneeling before him" (RSV), "bowing down" (NASB), "kneeling down" (NIV), "kneeling down" (NKJV), "kneeling before him" (ESV)*

1 Jn.5:7 For there are three that bear record in heaven, the Father, the Word, and the Holy Ghost: and these three are one. – *omitted in RSV, NASB, NIV, ESV*

The Virgin Birth of Christ

Isa. 7:14 ...Behold, a <u>virgin</u> shall conceive, and bear a son... – *"a young woman shall conceive" (RSV), "a young woman is with child" (REB)*

Lk. 2:33 And <u>Joseph</u> and his mother... – *"And his father and his mother" (RSV, ESV), "And his father and mother" (NASB), "The child's father and mother" (NIV)*

The Sinless Life of Christ

The Lord Jesus was angry with the unbelieving Jews (Mk. 3:5). The modern versions have Him condemning Himself with His own teaching by omitting, "without a cause" in Matt. 5:22 (RSV, NASB, NIV, ESV).

The Blood of Christ

Sinners are redeemed by the precious and pure blood of Christ. Why would any Bible omit references to the blood of Christ? For example, the vital words, "through his blood" (Col. 1:14) are omitted in the RSV, NASB, NIV, and ESV.

The Resurrection of Christ

Christ gave His apostles "many infallible proofs" of His bodily resurrection (Acts 1:3). Modern versions water this down: "many proofs" (RSV, ESV), "many convincing proofs" (NASB, NIV).

There are many other problems with the modern versions that we could point out.

Doctrines Attacked

1) Salvation – For example, the modern versions say that we are "being saved" (1 Cor. 1:18).
2) Scripture – Modern versions mess up key verses on the scripture (Ps. 12:6-7; 2 Cor. 2:17; 2 Tim. 3:16).
3) Study – Modern versions change "study" and "rightly dividing" (2 Tim. 2:15).

Errors in the Modern Versions

1) Who killed Goliath? We all know it was David, but the modern versions say it was Elhanan in 2 Samuel 21:19.

2) Is the quote in Mark 1:2 found in Isaiah like the modern versions say? No. The KJB says, "prophets" because Mark 1:2 quotes Malachi 3:1 and Mark 1:3 quotes Isaiah 40:3.
3) How many Israelites rebelled in the wilderness (Heb. 3:16-17)? The modern versions claim it was ALL that came out of Egypt. What about Caleb and Joshua?

Modern Versions Cast Doubt on the Word of God

Modern versions have footnotes that cast doubt on whole passages like Mark 16:9-20 and John 7:53-8:11. There are MANY whole and partial verses that are omitted in the modern versions.

Why So Many Versions?

Why have there been hundreds of Bible versions published in the last one hundred and twenty years? God is not the author of confusion (1 Cor. 14:33)! The publishers claim that they are producing new versions because they have access to better manuscripts, and that they want to make the Bible easier to understand. That is simply not true. They use corrupt manuscripts (2 Cor. 2:17). That the new versions are written in modern language does not mean they are easier to understand. It has been proven that the NIV is written on a higher reading level than the KJB. The average word In the KJB has five letters.

What are the real reasons?
1) Satan (Gen. 3:1)
2) Pride (multiple versions allow you to be your own authority)
3) The love of money (1 Tim. 6:10)

Wherefore by their fruits ye shall know them. (Matt. 7:20)

What have the modern versions produced as compared with the King James Bible? The KJB has been used of God for over four hundred years to build strong Christians and churches. The modern versions have produced liberalism and apostasy.

Be a Bible-Believer

Are you truly a Bible-believer? Do not expect the Spirit of God to illuminate your understanding of His word if you do not receive the Bible as being the very words of God.

For this cause also thank we God without ceasing, because, when ye received the word of God which ye heard of us, ye received it not as the word of men, but as it is in truth, the word of God, which effectually worketh also in you that believe. (1 Thess. 2:13)

Finally, brethren, pray for us, that the word of the Lord may have free course, and be glorified, even as it is with you: (2 Thess. 3:1)

Many preachers and teachers claim that the Bible was only inspired in the original manuscripts and preserved in the original languages. That would be a real problem for us since we do not have the original manuscripts or know the original languages. Thankfully, the Bible itself says no such thing. Men claim that a translation cannot be inspired, and yet the Bible provides many examples of inspired translations.

For the scripture saith unto Pharaoh, Even for this same purpose have I raised thee up, that I might shew my power in thee, and that my name might be declared throughout the all the earth. (Rom. 9:17)

What Moses said to Pharaoh is called "scripture" even though it was translated from Hebrew to Egyptian, written in Hebrew, translated into Greek, and now we have it in English.

Does it not make sense that in this present age in which God is building His church with predominately Gentile members that He would preserve His word in the language that most Gentiles speak? More people know English than any other language in the world.

If we believe what the Bible says about itself, we will believe that there is a perfect copy of God's inspired words available for us today. Timothy had inspired scripture because it had been preserved (2 Tim. 3:14-17). God promised to preserve His pure words "for ever" (Ps. 12:6-7). Where are they today? Those who do not believe the KJB do not believe any Bible is perfect. They claim to believe that God created the heaven and earth but find it hard to believe that He can give us a perfect Bible in English. No matter what men may say, the word of God lives and abides forever (1 Pet. 1:23).

Believing the Bible is foundational to rightly dividing it.

Study to shew thyself approved unto God, a workman that needeth not to be ashamed, rightly dividing the word of truth. (2 Tim. 2:15)

Study Notes

Do your best to present yourself to God as one approved, a worker who does not need to be ashamed and who correctly handles the word of truth. (2 Tim. 2:15, NIV)

No wonder the readers of the modern versions are ignorant of dispensational truth! They remove the command to rightly divide the word of truth.

Here are some examples (of many) that demonstrate how dispensational truth is lost in the modern versions. We will elaborate on the importance of these points throughout this book.

- The word "dispensation" appears four times in the KJB (1 Cor. 9:17; Eph. 1:10; 3:2; Col. 1:25), but it has been removed from the modern versions.
- The main division in the Bible is seen by comparing Acts 3:21 with Rom. 16:25. The NIV removes the key words "spoken" and "secret" from these verses.
- Justification by the "faith of Christ" (Gal. 2:16) – the modern versions remove this doctrine by changing it to *"faith in Christ."*
- Peter and Paul preached different gospels (Gal. 2:7) – the modern versions change it to *"gospel TO the..."* as though it was the same message but just to different groups.
- They conflate the prophesied baptism WITH the Holy Ghost with the baptism BY the Spirit into the Body of Christ by referring to both as baptism "in the Spirit" (cf. Acts 1:5; 1 Cor. 12:13).
- There is a difference between Israel and the new creature (Gal. 6:15-16) – the NIV calls the new creature the Israel of God in v.16.

Beware of preachers and teachers who try to rightly divide without believing they have the word of truth. It will not be long, and they will stop rightly dividing it because rejecting the inspiration of scripture is the first step in apostasy. The Bible is the sole authority in all matters of faith and practice. The importance of believing every word of God cannot be overemphasized.

5 Every word of God is pure: he is a shield unto them that put their trust in him.
6 Add thou not unto his words, lest he reprove thee, and thou be found a liar. (Prov. 30:5-6)

Chapter 4
Nine Rules for Fruitful Bible Study

As we saw in the previous chapters, two essential prerequisites for Bible study are (1) knowing that you are saved, and (2) being a Bible-believer. Once that has been established, following these nine rules will produce fruitful Bible study. The number nine is associated with fruitfulness in the Bible (e.g., see the nine-fold fruit of the Spirit in Gal. 5:22-23).

1) **We are to take the words of the scripture in their normal and literal sense.**

So they read in the book in the law of God distinctly, and gave the sense, and caused them to understand the reading. (Neh. 8:8)

The Bible contains figures of speech, but most of it is written in plain and literal language. We must always take the words in their normal and literal sense unless it is clearly impossible to do so. For example, when Christ said, "I am the door" (Jn. 10:9), He was obviously not saying that He is a literal door on hinges. Words have meaning, but the allegorical approach claims that the Bible does not mean what it says. This approach attacks the clarity, authority, and integrity of God's word.

2) **The scriptures are self-interpreting.**

Knowing this first, that no prophecy of the scripture is of any private interpretation. (2 Pet. 1:20)

It is not man's place to interpret God's word. There is only one right interpretation for every passage of scripture. The living word of God interprets itself as we study it God's way.

3) We must compare spiritual things with spiritual.

Which things also we speak, not in the words which man's wisdom teacheth, but which the Holy Ghost teacheth; comparing spiritual things with spiritual. (1 Cor. 2:13)

We must "search the scriptures" because one verse or passage will shed more light on another. Learning how to run cross-references is essential to Bible study. We must never seek to build a doctrine on an isolated text.

4) We must understand the difference between interpretation and application.

Interpretation is the right and proper explanation of what is written. It is to expound (i.e., unfold or open) the text in strict accordance with its context (Lk. 24:27, 44-45). Application is taking the moral principles found throughout the word of God and applying them to our daily walk (e.g., Rom. 15:4). Every passage of scripture has only one right interpretation, but it may have more than one application. We must not confuse a secondary application for the primary interpretation of a passage.

5) The King James Bible has its own built-in dictionary.

Words in the Bible can be understood by studying the Bible itself. There is no need to look to outside sources to understand Bible words. There is nothing wrong with consulting a good dictionary (e.g., Webster's 1828 Dictionary), but we must not rely on man-made definitions first and foremost to understand Bible words.

Guidelines with examples:
1. Look up the first mention of the word because it *typically* sets the tone for how the word is used in the Bible (e.g., repented in Gen. 6:5-7).
2. Consider the word in context, note other words nearby (e.g., asswaged in Gen. 8:1-5).
3. Note parallelism – (e.g., the parallels in 2 Cor. 6:14-16 teach us that fellowship is having communion, concord, part, and agreement).
4. Check cross-references (e.g., anon defined as immediately by comparing Matt. 13:20 with Mk. 4:16).

6) Context, Context, Context!

The Bible is not a collection of sayings. All false teachers use the Bible, but they use it out of context. Consider each passage in light of its dispensational context. What is the context of the book? What is the context of the chapter? What is the immediate context?

7) We must always keep in mind that the scriptures were given by progressive revelation.

A biblical dispensation is marked by God dispensing new revelation that brings about a major change in how He deals with man. We must not read truth back into a passage before it was revealed. For example, the baptism WITH the Holy Ghost in Acts 2 according to prophecy (Acts 2:16) cannot be the same baptism BY the Spirit into the Body of Christ which was a mystery later revealed through Paul (1 Cor. 12:13).

8) We must consider what Paul says first.

Consider what I say; and the Lord give thee understanding in all things. (2 Tim. 2:7)

Since the apostle Paul is the divinely appointed spokesman for this present age, we must consider what he says first if we are going to understand the scriptures. We cannot possibly follow everything the Bible says because sometimes it gives different sets of instructions concerning the same issue. We must follow the doctrine Christ gave through the apostle Paul for this present age (1 Cor. 4:16-17; 11:1).

9) We must rightly divide the word of truth.

Study to shew thyself approved unto God, a workman that needeth not to be ashamed, rightly dividing the word of truth. (2 Tim. 2:15)

This is the main key to Bible study. In the one verse in which God told us to study His word, He told us exactly how to do it. The remainder of this book will expound upon this main key.

Chapter 5
The Basics of Dispensational Truth

God does not change in His person, principles, or promises (Mal. 3:6; Heb. 13:8), but He certainly does change in His dealings with man (Heb. 1:1). If you do not recognize this fact, the Bible will be a confusing book to you because we cannot possibly obey all of the instructions found within its pages.

Consider the basic issue of what we are to eat:
1) Adam (Gen. 1:29) – no meat
2) Noah (Gen. 9:3-4) – meat without blood
3) Moses (Lev. 11:46-47) – only "clean" meats
4) Paul (1 Tim. 4:1-5) – nothing is to be refused

We must understand the difference between moral truth and dispensational truth. There are moral principles that never change. For example, murder is a sin in every dispensation. The sabbath day is an example of dispensational truth. God gave Israel sabbaths to observe, but He never gave them to the Body of Christ (Col. 2:16). The moral truth of the law still applies today. The apostle Paul reaffirmed nine of the ten commandments (e.g., Rom. 13:8-10).

All scripture is profitable for us, but we will not gain the profit that God has for us in His word unless we study it His way.

All scripture is given by inspiration of God and is profitable for doctrine, for reproof, for correction, for instruction in righteousness: (2 Tim. 3:16)

Study to shew thyself approved unto God, a workman that needeth not to be ashamed, rightly dividing the word of truth. (2 Tim. 2:15)

Note three things in this key verse:
1) **The Mandate** – *What we are to do* – "Study"
2) **The Motive** – *Why we are to do it* – "to shew thyself approved unto God"
3) **The Method** – *How we are to do it* – "rightly dividing the word of truth"

Rightly dividing the word of truth is not an issue of dividing truth from error because there are no errors in the Bible. It is an issue of recognizing and consistently maintaining the divisions that God put in His word. What was truth for Israel under the law may not be truth for the Body of Christ under grace. This is the dispensational approach to Bible study.

The context of 2 Timothy 2:15 interprets what it means to rightly divide the word of truth.

(16) But shun profane *and* vain babblings: for they will increase unto more ungodliness.
(17) And their word will eat as doth a canker: of whom is Hymenaeus and Philetus;
(18) Who concerning the truth have erred, saying that the resurrection is past already; and overthrow the faith of some. (2 Tim. 2:16-18)

Notice that Hymenaeus and Philetus did not deny the truth of the resurrection but failed to rightly divide it and thus put it in the wrong place.

All Bible students divide the Bible to some extent, but most do not rightly divide it. We must be careful not to **invent** our own divisions or **ignore** the ones that God placed in His word.

There has always been an attack on dispensationalism. Many simply do not understand the matter which is proven by how they misrepresent it. For example, opponents of dispensationalism accuse us of chopping up the Bible and only regarding Paul's epistles as being essential. The truth is we believe the whole Bible and we are not exalting Paul, but simply acknowledging that God chose him to be the pattern and spokesman for this present age of grace (1 Cor. 11:1; 1 Tim. 1:16). It is not about Paul *as a man*, but what Christ revealed through him for us.

One Book Rightly Divided

The Bible is one book made up of many different books. It has unity and diversity, as its Author who is one God in three persons (1 Jn. 5:7). God used about forty different writers from various backgrounds and locations over a period of about fifteen hundred years to write the sixty-six books of the Bible. These books cover about seven thousand years of human history and give glimpses into eternity past and future. The Bible is not everything God knows, but it is everything He wants us to know about Him and His plan and purpose for the ages. That sixty-six books make up one book without error or contradiction proves that the Bible is given by inspiration of God.

There are 1,189 chapters, 31,102 verses, and 783,137 words in the King James Bible. Not only did God inspire and preserve His words so that we have a perfect copy of it today in our own language, but He also led men in the proper arrangement of its books as well the chapter and verse divisions so that the Bible is laid out in a divine order perfectly designed for our edification. Chapter and verse divisions greatly enhance our ability to search the scriptures.

The Bible is an inexhaustible gold mine of divine revelation. We could spend a lifetime studying it in detail and never learn it all, but we should seek to learn as much as possible. The purpose of learning the Bible is not about just gaining knowledge, but the knowledge of God. The Bible is God's perfect revelation of Himself to man. God preserved the whole Bible for us because we need all of it (2 Tim. 3:16).

The Unity of the Bible

- It reveals one true and living God.
- It reveals one main purpose – the glory of God.
- It reveals one main theme – the person and work of Christ (Jn. 5:39).
- It reveals one main goal – the establishment of God's kingdom in heaven and earth.
- It reveals one plan of redemption – by the blood of Christ (Heb. 9:22).
- It reveals one set of moral principles – God's moral principles never change.
- It reveals one main enemy – Satan (Gen. 3:1; Rev. 12:9).

- It reveals a harmonious unfolding of progressive revelation – there are changes, but no real contradictions when the Bible is rightly divided.

Divisions in the Bible

It is the failure to acknowledge the divisions God put in His word that is the root cause of all manner of heresies.

A twofold division:

Prophecy (Acts 3:21)	**Mystery (Rom. 16:25)**
Earth (Ex. 19:5-6)	Heaven (Eph. 2:6)
From the foundation of the world (Matt. 25:34)	Before the foundation of the world (Eph. 1:4)
Christ the King - Israel over the Gentiles (Isa. 60:1-3)	Christ the Head of one Body - neither Jew nor Gentile (Col. 3:11)

A threefold division:
1) **Time Past** (Eph. 2:11-12) – Genesis through early Acts – God made a distinction between the Circumcision and Uncircumcision (e.g., Matt. 15:21-28)
2) **But Now** (Eph. 2:13-18) – Romans through Philemon – God makes no difference between Jews and Gentiles (1 Cor. 12:13; Gal. 3:27-28)
3) **Ages to Come** (Eph. 2:6-7) – Hebrews through Revelation – The difference resumes, Israel reigns on earth (Rev. 5:10) but the Body of Christ in heavenly places

A six-fold division concerning the King and His Kingdom:
1) Old Testament – Promised and prophesied
2) Gospels – Presented and rejected

3) Acts – Reoffered and rejected (Acts 1-7), transition period (Acts 8-28)
4) Pauline Epistles – Postponed, the mystery of one Body revealed
5) Hebrew Epistles – Resumed and proclaimed
6) Revelation – Established

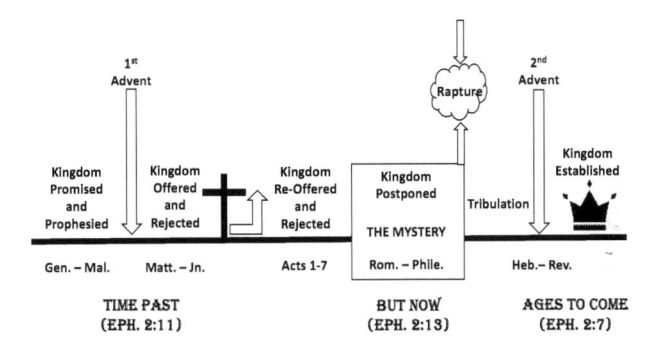

1st Advent			Rapture	2nd Advent
Kingdom Promised and Prophesied	Kingdom Offered and Rejected	Kingdom Re-Offered and Rejected	Kingdom Postponed THE MYSTERY	Tribulation / Kingdom Established
Gen. – Mal.	Matt. – Jn.	Acts 1-7	Rom. – Phile.	Heb. – Rev.
TIME PAST (EPH. 2:11)			BUT NOW (EPH. 2:13)	AGES TO COME (EPH. 2:7)

Dispensations

There are different dispensations revealed in the word of God. The word "dispensation" is used four times in the Bible by the apostle Paul (1 Cor. 9:17; Eph. 1:10; 3:2; Col. 1:25). A dispensation is a dealing out, distribution, or dispensing of something.

The Bible was given by progressive revelation. A biblical dispensation is a dispensing of divine revelation. It is a particular way that God deals with man. It is an administration or stewardship. Dispensations are not periods of time. Ages are periods of time (Eph. 2:7; 3:5), but dispensations operate within ages.

A biblical dispensation is marked by five things:
1) Divine revelation – which brings about clear changes in God's dealings with men.
2) Human spokesman – for example, Moses for the law and Paul for the mystery.
3) Human responsibility to the revelation – man must be tested.
4) Human failure – every dispensation ends in apostasy except for the last one.
5) Divine judgment – there is no remedy for apostasy.

By following these five marks of a biblical dispensation, we may identify seven dispensations in human history with the eighth and final dispensation being the eternal state when God's purposes as revealed in the times of human history will have finally come to fulness (Eph. 1:10). In the Bible, seven is God's number of perfection and eight is the number of a new beginning.

It is important to understand that dispensations are not cut-and-dried periods of time and that there is overlapping and transitions in dispensational truth.

Transitional books:
- Matthew – from prophecy to fulfillment
- Acts – from law to grace; Israel to the Body of Christ; Peter to Paul
- Hebrews – from the old covenant to the new covenant; from tribulation to the Kingdom Age

By gaining a basic understanding of the different dispensations, we also gain a general framework of the whole Bible.

Overview of the Dispensations in Human History

I. Innocence (Gen. 1-3)
A. Revelation – Man was created in the image of God and given dominion on the earth. God placed the man and woman in a perfect garden and told them to be fruitful, and multiply, and replenish the earth.
B. Spokesman – God.
C. Responsibility – Adam was to dress and keep the garden. He could eat of every tree except the tree of the knowledge of good and evil. Given a free will, man had to be tested.
D. Failure – The woman was deceived by the serpent and ate of the tree of the knowledge of good and evil. The man obeyed his wife instead of God (Rom. 5:12).
E. Judgment – The man and woman were cursed and expelled from the garden. The serpent and the ground were also cursed.

II. Conscience (Gen. 4-8)
A. Revelation – Man now operates with a personal and experimental knowledge of good and evil- of good as obedience, of evil as disobedience to the known will of God (Rom. 1:19; 2:14-15). God revealed the necessity for a blood sacrifice to cover sins (Gen. 4:1-8). There was no written law (Rom. 5:13-14).
B. Spokesman – Adam, who lived 930 years, was a firsthand witness of creation and the fall.
C. Responsibility – Choose the good and refuse the evil, offer a blood sacrifice for sin (Gen. 4:7).
D. Failure – World-wide corruption (Gen. 6:1-8).
E. Judgment – A universal flood.

Study Notes

III. Human Government (Gen. 9-11)
A. Revelation – Man is to be governed by man (Gen. 9:1-7).
B. Spokesman – Noah.
C. Responsibility – Government led by mankind, then Israel, then "times of the Gentiles" (Lk. 21:24).
D. Failure – Babel (Rom. 1:18-32); Israel breaking the law covenant; Babylonian system.
E. Judgment – Confusion of tongues at Babel; Israel lost her kingdom; the Day of the LORD.

IV. Promise (Gen. 12 - Ex. 19)
A. Revelation – The Abrahamic covenant.
B. Spokesman – Abraham.
C. Responsibility – The patriarchs were to trust God to fulfill His promises.
D. Failure – Unbelief and disobedience by Abraham, Isaac, Jacob and his twelve sons.
E. Judgment – The children of Israel became slaves in Egypt.

V. Law (Ex. 20 – early Acts)
A. Revelation – The law and land covenants (Deut. 29:1).
B. Spokesman – Moses.
C. Responsibility – Obey and be blessed in the land or disobey and be cursed and eventually dispersed from the land.
D. Failure – Breaking the covenants; rejection of Father (OT), Son (Gospels), and Spirit (early Acts).
E. Judgment – Assyrian and Babylonian captivities; the dispersion; Israel falls in Acts 7.

VI. Mystery (Rom. - Phile.)
A. Revelation – The Body of Christ and corresponding mysteries (1 Cor. 4:1; Eph. 3:1-13).
B. Spokesman – Paul (Rom. 11:13).
C. Responsibility – Follow Paul's example and doctrine (1 Cor. 4:16; 11:1; Phil. 3:17; 4:9; 2 Tim. 2:7).
D. Failure – Apostasy from Paul's message (1 Tim. 4:1; 2 Tim. 1:15; 3:1, 5; 4:3-4).
E. Judgment – The Judgment Seat of Christ (1 Cor. 3:10-17; 2 Cor. 5:10).

VII. Kingdom (Heb. - Rev.)
A. Revelation – The kingdom of heaven is once again "at hand" in Hebrews through Revelation. Christ will be King in Jerusalem reigning over the whole earth. Israel will teach the nations God's law (Isa. 2:1-5).
B. Spokesman – Christ (Heb. 1:2); secondarily: Peter, James, and John (Matt. 17:1).
C. Responsibility – Obey the King.
D. Failure – The final battle with Satan (Rev. 20:7-8).
E. Judgment – The heavens and earth dissolved with fire and the last judgment (Rev. 20:9-15).

The apostle Paul referred to all eight dispensations:
1) Innocence (1 Cor. 15:45-47; 1 Tim. 2:13-14)
2) Conscience (Rom. 1:19; 2:14-15)
3) Human Government (Rom. 13:1-7)
4) Promise (Gal. 3:16-18)
5) Law (Gal. 3:19-23)
6) Grace, or Mystery (Eph. 3:1-7; Col. 1:24-27)
7) Kingdom (1 Cor. 15:24-28)
8) Fulness of Times (Eph. 1:9-10)

Chapter 6
The Apostle Paul

In His earthly ministry, Christ said to His disciples, "Follow me" (Matt. 4:19). The only other man in the Bible who plainly tells people to follow his example and teaching is the apostle Paul.

Be ye followers of me, even as I also am of Christ.
(1 Cor. 11:1)

One of the most important truths that believers need to learn is that Paul is the divinely appointed pattern and spokesman for the Body of Christ to follow in this present age of grace (1 Cor. 4:16-17; Phil. 3:17-21; 4:9). Sadly, very few churches today recognize this truth, which is not surprising in light of the fact many were already departing from it in the first century (2 Tim. 1:15).

In saying that we are to follow Paul, we are simply quoting scripture. We are not exalting a man or making more out of Paul than the scripture does. We are certainly not putting Christ and Paul on the same level. We know that Paul was the "chief of sinners" saved by grace, while Christ is the sinless Son of God and the Saviour of sinners. We know that Paul was nothing in himself while Christ is everything for "in him dwelleth all the fulness of the Godhead bodily" (Col. 2:9). But it was to Paul that the glorified Lord committed the revelation of His message and program for this present dispensation.

It is not the person but the office of Paul that we magnify (Rom. 11:13). Paul rebuked the carnal Corinthians for following him as a man (1 Cor. 1:10-17). We are to follow the DOCTRINE that Christ revealed through Paul (1 Tim. 1:3; 6:3; 2 Tim. 1:13; 2:2; 3:10-14).

Even though the word of God plainly tells believers in this present age to follow the apostle Paul, many professing Christians resent that idea when presented with it and claim to follow the whole Bible instead. However, that is not possible because God's word has different things to say to different groups living under different dispensations. Even a casual reading of the Bible will reveal that there are different instructions given concerning the same issues.

All of the Bible is the word of God and is therefore profitable FOR us (2 Tim. 3:16), but it is not all written directly TO us (2 Tim. 2:15). We need to read and study the whole Bible. When we come across something that does not line up with what the apostle Paul taught in his epistles, we are to follow what Christ said through Paul directly to us in this present age (1 Tim. 6:3; 2 Tim. 2:7).

We are not pitting the words of Moses, Jesus Christ, or Peter against Paul. All scripture is given by inspiration of God and is therefore the word of God. But the word of God must be rightly divided if it is going to be understood.

In rightly dividing the word of truth, we must recognize the difference between the ministries of the apostle Paul and the twelve apostles. Yet, mainstream dispensationalists insist that there is no difference between the ministries of Peter and Paul and claim that it is "hyper-dispensationalism" to believe that there is. They have evidently never asked themselves the important question, "Why Paul?" If his apostleship, message, and ministry were the same as the twelve apostles, what was the point of Christ saving him in the manner He did, away from Jerusalem, and away from the twelve apostles?

Why Paul?

The twelve apostles had already been commissioned by Christ to go into all the world (Mk. 16:15). They did not go, but Paul did (Col. 1:6). What brought about this change? It was the continued rejection of Christ by the leaders of Israel, their fall, and the subsequent revelation of the mystery (Rom. 16:25).

In the kingdom commission, the apostles were instructed to begin at Jerusalem because according to prophecy the Gentiles are to be blessed through Israel, and Jerusalem will be the capitol city in the Kingdom Age (Jer. 3:17). Because the nation of Israel did not repent of killing their Messiah, there was no need for them to go to the nations. When Paul explained his ministry to the apostles in Jerusalem (Gal. 2:1-10), they agreed that he would go to the heathen with his gospel while they continued to go to the circumcision. The commission given to the twelve apostles was postponed, but it will be fulfilled in the future tribulation period (Matt. 24:14).

Paul's ministry was so different from the twelve apostles that some to this very day claim that he was a false apostle. Even lost people can see a difference between Peter and Paul.

It is not an exaggeration to say that Paul's conversion is one of the most significant events in the Bible.

- It is more fully described and more often referred to than any other conversion.
- It is more fully described and more often referred to than any other personal experience in the Bible outside the crucifixion and resurrection of Christ.
- The majority of three chapters in Acts are taken up with the account of it (9, 22, 26).
- So aware was Paul himself of the significance of his conversion that he refers to it repeatedly in his epistles (1 Cor. 15:8-10; Gal. 1:11-23; Phil. 3:4-11; 1 Tim. 1:12-17). He wrote by inspiration of God. Clearly, the Lord has placed an emphasis on the distinct apostleship and ministry of Paul because he is the spokesman for the Body of Christ to follow in this present age.

The Apostle Paul is Distinct from the Twelve Apostles

1) Distinct Conversion

The sudden and glorious appearance of Christ to Saul of Tarsus (Acts 9) was totally off the prophetic script. He had blasphemed the Holy Ghost (Acts 7:51-60) and therefore could not be saved under the gospel of the kingdom (Matt. 12:31-32). Everything was ripe and ready for God's wrath to poured out (Acts 7:56), but instead He poured out exceeding abundant grace by saving the leader of the rebellion against Him (1 Tim. 1:12-17) and sending him out with the message of reconciliation that He might build one NEW man, the church which is the Body of Christ (Eph.

2:11-18). Paul was the first one to receive the gospel of Christ (Gal. 1:11-12).

2) Distinct Apostleship

All of the apostles saw the Lord and were personally sent out by Him with a message and ministry (with the "signs of an apostle"). Paul clearly distinguished his apostleship from that of the twelve (Rom. 11:13; 1 Cor. 15:5; Gal. 1-2). He was not even qualified to be one of the twelve apostles, and there are many differences between his apostleship and theirs.

3) Distinct Message

Paul received an abundance of revelations (2 Cor. 12:7) directly from the Lord. The gospel of the grace of God (Acts 20:24; Gal. 1:11-12), the church which is the Body of Christ (Eph. 3:1-13), the rapture of the Body of Christ (1 Cor. 15:51), and many other things were revealed to him first. He was the first one to glory in the cross and preach it as good news (Gal. 6:14). It is Paul alone who taught that we are justified by the faith of Christ (Gal. 2:16). It is Paul alone who says, "ye are not under the law, but under grace" (Rom. 6:14-15).

4) Distinct Commission

When we simply compare how Christ sent out the twelve apostles with how He sent out Paul, it should be obvious that they were not sent under the same commission.

The 12	Paul
Sent by Christ on earth (Acts 1:8-9)	Sent by Christ from heaven (Acts 26:19)
Begin in Jerusalem (Lk. 24:47)	Depart from Jerusalem (Acts 22:21)
Gospel of the kingdom (Matt. 24:14)	Gospel of the grace of God (Acts 20:24)
Go baptize (Matt. 28:19)	Sent not to baptize (1 Cor. 1:17)
Teach the law (Matt. 28:20)	Not under the law (Rom. 6:14)

Distinct Ministry

Having a different apostleship, message, and commission means that Paul had a different ministry. He was "made a minister" to every creature with the gospel of the grace of God, and to the church which is the Body of Christ with the mystery (Col. 1:24-29). Are there some similarities between Peter and Paul? Yes, but for every similarity there are significant differences. Why does it matter? We cannot follow the ministries of both Peter and Paul at the same time in light of the differences between their doctrine. Who are we to follow? We are to follow Paul because He is divinely appointed pattern and spokesman for this present age of grace. This is the answer for all of the confusion that abounds in the professing church today.

Paul was not one of the Twelve Apostles

Some Bible teachers claim that Paul was God's choice to replace Judas Iscariot, and therefore Peter was out of God's will when he led in appointing Matthias as the replacement (Acts 1:15-26).

(15) And in those days Peter stood up in the midst of the disciples, and said, (the number of names together were about an hundred and twenty,)

(16) Men *and* brethren, this scripture must needs have been fulfilled, which the Holy Ghost by the mouth of David spake before concerning Judas, which was guide to them that took Jesus.

(17) For he was numbered with us, and had obtained part of this ministry.

(18) Now this man purchased a field with the reward of iniquity; and falling headlong, he burst asunder in the midst, and all his bowels gushed out.

(19) And it was known unto all the dwellers at Jerusalem; insomuch as that field is called in their proper tongue, Aceldama, that is to say, The field of blood.

(20) For it is written in the book of Psalms, Let his habitation be desolate, and let no man dwell therein: and his bishoprick let another take.

(21) Wherefore of these men which have companied with us all the time that the Lord Jesus went in and out among us,

(22) Beginning from the baptism of John, unto that same day that he was taken up from us, must one be ordained to be a witness with us of his resurrection.

(23) And they appointed two, Joseph called Barsabas, who was surnamed Justus, and Matthias.

(24) And they prayed, and said, Thou, Lord, which knowest the hearts of all *men,* shew whether of these two thou hast chosen,

(25) That he may take part of this ministry and apostleship, from which Judas by transgression fell, that he might go to his own place.

(26) And they gave forth their lots; and the lot fell upon Matthias; and he was numbered with the eleven apostles. (Acts 1:15-26)

The following points prove that Matthias was the divinely appointed replacement for Judas.

1) It was prophesied that another would take the place of Judas (Ps. 109:8), but Paul's special ministry had to do with a mystery hid from the prophets (Col. 1:24-27).
2) There had to be twelve apostles for the kingdom to be offered to Israel in the early Acts period (Matt. 19:28).
3) Peter and the other apostles had the authority to act in the stead of Christ (Matt. 16:19; 18:18-19).
4) They prayed about the matter (Acts 1:24), and Christ promised to give them whatsoever they asked (Matt. 21:22).
5) Some think casting lots was a wrong thing to do (Acts 1:26), but it was a scriptural way for the Jews to discern God's will (Prov. 16:33).
6) Paul did not meet the qualifications to be one of the twelve (Acts 1:21-22).
7) The apostles were "filled with the Holy Ghost" a few days later (Acts 2:4).
8) Matthias was "numbered with the eleven apostles," and the Holy Spirit stated that Peter stood up "with the eleven" (Acts 2:14).
9) Paul was not appointed through men, but by God Himself (Gal. 1:1).

There are clear differences between the ministries of Paul and the twelve apostles. Paul plainly and purposely distinguished himself from them. While there were other apostles that the Lord sent from heaven to the Body of Christ (Eph. 4:8-12), Paul was "THE apostle of the Gentiles" (Rom. 11:13).

1) The twelve were chosen by Christ on earth. Israel is God's earthly people (Deut. 7:6). Paul was chosen by Christ from heaven. The Body of Christ is God's heavenly people (Eph. 2:6).
2) The twelve were appointed to lead Israel (Matt. 19:28). Paul was appointed to lead the Body of Christ (Col. 1:24-27).
3) The twelve represent the twelve tribes of Israel. Paul represents the one Body of Christ. He was a "Hebrew of the Hebrews." and yet he was also a Roman citizen (Phil. 3:5; Acts 22:27-28). So, in a sense, we could say that he was a Jew and Gentile in one body.
4) The twelve only knew Christ on earth. When Christ ascended back to heaven, a cloud received Him out of their sight (Acts 1:9). Paul only knew Christ from heaven (Acts 26:16).
5) The twelve were sent to proclaim and offer the kingdom of heaven to Israel (Matt. 10:5-7; Acts 3:19-21). Paul was sent to preach the gospel of the grace of God (Acts 20:24).
6) The ministry of the twelve was based on covenants and prophecy (Acts 3:24-25). After Israel is blessed, the Gentiles receive blessings through them. The ministry of Paul was based on a mystery. The Gentiles are blessed through the fall of Israel (Rom. 11:11) and there is neither Jew nor Gentile in the Body of Christ (Gal. 3:27-28).
7) Under the kingdom commission water baptism was required and signs were the evidence of salvation (Mk. 16:15-18). Under Paul's commission he was not sent to

baptize, and he said early in his ministry that signs would cease (1 Cor. 1:17; 13:8-10).

Magnifying Paul's Office

The apostle Paul had something to say about the importance of his message and ministry in every epistle that he wrote. He gave all glory to God and knew that he was nothing as a man (Rom. 7:18). He considered himself to be, the least of the apostles (1 Cor. 15:9-10), less than the least of all saints (Eph. 3:8), and the chief of sinners (1 Tim. 1:15).

Yet, he knew that God, by His exceeding abundant grace, had given him a special ministry.

For I speak to you Gentiles, inasmuch as I am the apostle of the Gentiles, I magnify mine office: (Rom. 11:13)

Why do so many preachers try to minimize what God has magnified? Sadly, they magnify tradition over the truth of God's word.

I will worship toward thy holy temple, and praise thy name for thy lovingkindness and for thy truth: for thou hast magnified thy word above all thy name. (Ps. 138:2)

What good is God's name if He cannot keep His word? How many preachers in the world today believe that God inspired and perfectly preserved His words? Very few. Among those that believe that, how many recognize Paul as the pattern and spokesman for the Body of Christ to follow in this present age of grace? Even fewer.

Do we make too much out of Paul? Let's consider what the word of God says about his ministry.

1) Apostle (Gal. 1:1)

That God inspired Paul to write much scripture in defense of his apostleship proves the importance of it. His apostleship was under constant attack largely because of the distinctiveness of his message and ministry. Apostles were men chosen by the Lord and personally sent out by Him with a message and signs to confirm it (2 Cor. 12:12). While on earth, Christ sent twelve apostles to the twelve tribes of Israel. From heaven, He sent Paul and other apostles to the Body of Christ. With the completion of the word of God there is no longer a need for apostles. Paul was the last one to see the Lord (1 Cor. 15:8). Christ sent him as the apostle to the Gentiles and the Body of Christ (Acts 26:16-18). There are some who say they will not follow Paul because they follow the Lord. You cannot follow the Lord if you do not follow the apostle that He sent to you (Jn. 13:20).

2) Preacher (1 Tim. 2:3-7)

As a preacher, Paul faithfully heralded the gospel that Christ revealed to him and committed to his trust (2 Tim. 4:16-17; Titus 1:1-3). Christ sent Paul to preach the gospel (1 Cor. 1:17) and His unsearchable riches (Eph. 3:8). He was the greatest evangelist the world has ever known.

3) Teacher (2 Tim. 1:11)

As a teacher, Paul faithfully taught the doctrines that Christ revealed through him for the Body of Christ in this present age and trained faithful men to teach others also (1 Cor. 4:15-17; 2 Tim. 2:2).

4) Minister (Col. 1:21-29)

He was a minister to every creature with the gospel and to the church with the mystery. Paul was not a Christian celebrity, but a humble servant of the Lord (1 Thess. 2:6). He did not abuse his great authority (2 Cor. 1:24).

5) Ambassador (Eph. 6:19-20)

Ambassadors are sent with a message (Prov. 13:17) to a foreign land (Phil. 3:20) in a time of peace (2 Cor. 6:2) to represent their king (1 Tim. 1:17). Christ revealed the mystery of the gospel to Paul (Gal. 1:11-12), and he became a prisoner of the Lord by faithfully fulfilling his ministry. All members of the Body of Christ are ambassadors for Christ (2 Cor. 5:17-21).

6) Pattern (1 Tim. 1:12-16)

Paul is our pattern in salvation in that he was saved by grace through faith in the finished work of Christ. He is also our example in how to walk and serve the Lord (Phil. 4:9).

7) Wise Masterbuilder (1 Cor. 3:10-11)

Paul laid the foundation for this present age by preaching Christ according to the revelation of the mystery (Rom. 16:25). Christ gave him the blueprints, so to speak, for how to do the work of the ministry in this present age.

8) Steward (1 Cor. 4:1-2)

Christ revealed the great mystery (i.e., secret) of the Body of Christ as well as other corresponding mysteries to Paul, and he was a faithful steward of those mysteries.

9) Spokesman (1 Cor. 14:37)

Paul did not use the word "spokesman," but it is a Bible word for someone who speaks for another (Ex. 4:16). Paul was God's mouthpiece to the Gentiles and the Body of Christ. God took Moses up on a mount and revealed the law through him for Israel. After his conversion, Paul went out into the wilderness for three years (likely on the same mount) to receive revelations for this present age for the Body of Christ (Gal. 1:15-20). Paul's thirteen epistles are the word of God. Just as it was apostasy for Israel to depart from Moses as God's spokesman for the law, so it is apostasy today for the church to depart from Paul as God's spokesman for this present dispensation (2 Tim. 1:13-15; 4:3-4).

Chapter 7
Mysteries in the Bible

The word of God was given by progressive revelation over a period of about fifteen hundred years. New revelation that brought about major changes in God's dealings with man is dispensational truth. Moses, who wrote the five books of the law, knew that God had secret things that He had yet to reveal.

The secret things belong unto the LORD our God: but those things which are revealed belong unto us and to our children for ever, that we may do all the words of this law. (Deut. 29:29)

God knows how to keep a secret! Nobody, not even the devil himself, can know the secrets of the Lord until He reveals them (Rom. 11:33). The secrets of the Lord concern both His purpose for heaven and earth.

(2) It is the glory of God to conceal a thing: but the honour of kings is to search out a matter.
(3) The <u>heaven</u> for height, and the <u>earth</u> for depth, and the heart of kings is unsearchable. (Prov. 25:2-3)

One of the main reasons God has kept secrets is because of the adversary. God's mysteries are revealed after apparent failure. Of course, God never fails but man always does.

(6) Howbeit we speak wisdom among them that are perfect: yet not the wisdom of this world, nor of the princes of this world, that come to nought:
(7) But we speak the wisdom of God in a mystery, *even* the hidden *wisdom,* which God ordained before the world unto our glory:
(8) Which none of the princes of this world knew: for had they known *it,* they would not have crucified the Lord of glory. (1 Cor. 2:6-8)

The words "mystery" and "mysteries" are found twenty-seven times in the Bible: three times in the Gospel records, twenty times in Paul's epistles, and four times in the book of Revelation. If you take the time to read all the references in context, you will learn that a mystery in the Bible is a secret that cannot be known until it is revealed.

Three Categories of Mysteries:
1) There are mysteries that concern the prophetic kingdom program of Israel that Christ revealed to His disciples on EARTH (Matt. 13:10-17, 34-35; Rev. 10:7).
2) There are mysteries concerning this present age that Christ revealed through the apostle Paul from HEAVEN (1 Cor. 4:1-2).
3) Satan has a mystery that works in opposition to what God is doing (2 Thess. 2:7; Rev. 2:24; 17:1-7).

Mysteries Concerning this Present Age

1) Israel's blindness (Rom. 11:25) – How this age began.
2) Body of Christ (Rom. 16:25; Eph. 3:1-13) – What this age is about.

3) The rapture of the Body of Christ (1 Cor. 15:51-52) – How this age will end.
4) God's will (Eph. 1:8-12) – Our role in the eternal state.
5) The Gospel (Eph. 6:19-20) – How to get in the Body of Christ.
6) Godliness (1 Tim. 3:16) – How to live as a member of Body of Christ.
7) Iniquity (2 Thess. 2:7) – How Satan opposes the mystery of godliness.

A Brief Commentary on Ephesians 3:1-13

(1) For this cause I Paul, the prisoner of Jesus Christ for you Gentiles,

It was Paul's ministry among the Gentiles that led to him becoming a prisoner (Acts 22:17-24). He considered himself a prisoner of Christ, not of Rome (Eph. 4:1; 2 Tim. 1:8; Phile. 1, 9), because he was in the will of God.

(2) If ye have heard of the dispensation of the grace of God which is given me to you-ward:

Yet here we are nearly two thousand years later, and the majority of professing Christians still have not heard of the dispensation of the grace of God that was given through Paul to the Gentiles! Satan has been working hard to keep people blinded to this truth. God dispensed the message of grace through Paul's ministry (1 Cor. 9:17; Col. 1:25), and the grace that he needed to make it known (Eph. 3:7-8). He needed much grace because he suffered much to fulfill his ministry.

(3) How that by revelation he made known unto me the mystery; (as I wrote afore in few words,
(4) Whereby, when ye read, ye may understand my knowledge in the mystery of Christ)
(5) Which in other ages was not made known unto the sons of men, as it is now revealed unto his holy apostles and prophets by the Spirit;

The risen and glorified Christ from heaven appeared to Paul in order to directly reveal the mystery to him. His knowledge in the mystery of Christ may be understood when we read the scriptures that he wrote by inspiration of God (2 Tim. 2:7). The mystery of the Body of Christ was kept secret in other ages, but it is now revealed to our understanding by the Spirit as we read what Paul wrote.

The "apostles and prophets" he referred to (v.5) were those whom Christ sent from heaven to minister to the Body of Christ (Eph. 4:8-12). The mystery was revealed to them "by the Spirit" when they heard Paul, which is a different thing than Christ personally revealing the mystery to Paul first.

(6) That the Gentiles should be fellowheirs, and of the same body, and partakers of his promise in Christ by the gospel:

That Gentiles would be blessed was not a mystery (Gen. 12:3). There are examples of it in the Old Testament (e.g., Ruth) and the prophets spoke of it (e.g., Isa. 60:1-5). The mystery that Christ revealed through Paul is that believing Gentiles would be fellowheirs (Eph. 1:11) in the SAME BODY.

According to prophecy the Gentiles are to be blessed through Israel's rise, but according to the mystery we are blessed through their fall (Rom. 11:11-15). Israel does not have a favored position above the Gentiles in this age. All believers are made members of the same spiritual Body (Eph. 2:13-18).

The Body of Christ is one new spiritual man in which there is neither Jew nor Gentile (Gal. 3:27-28). We become members of this Body "by the gospel." This is obviously referring to the gospel that Paul received by revelation of Jesus Christ (Gal. 1:11-12). We are made partakers of the Holy Spirit of promise when we believe Paul's gospel (Eph. 1:13).

Most Christians believe the Body of Christ began on the Day of Pentecost in Acts 2. How could the Body of Christ begin before the gospel that we must believe in order to be in the Body was revealed?

(7) Whereof I was made a minister, according to the gift of the grace of God given unto me by the effectual working of his power.

The apostle Paul was given a twofold ministry: to every creature with the gospel (Col. 1:23) and to the Body of Christ with the mystery (Col. 1:24-29). He was able to finish his course (2 Tim. 4:7) by the grace and power of God.

(8) Unto me, who am less than the least of all saints, is this grace given, that I should preach among the Gentiles the unsearchable riches of Christ;

Paul magnified his office as the apostle to the Gentiles (Rom. 11:13), but he knew that as a man he was nothing (Rom. 7:18). He knew that he did not deserve to be an apostle (1 Cor. 15:10) and considered himself to be "less than the least of all saints." His ministry was totally by the grace of God. The unsearchable riches of Christ concern spiritual truth that cannot be found by searching the Old Testament or fully grasped by the human mind.

(9) And to make all men see what is the fellowship of the mystery, which from the beginning of the world hath been hid in God, who created all things by Jesus Christ:

The "fellowship of the mystery" is our unity as the Body of Christ (Eph. 4:1-6). The goal of Paul's ministry was to make all men see this blessed truth, but sadly most believers today seem to be blinded to it.

The mystery was not hidden in the Old Testament. It was "hid in God." No one knew it until God revealed it through Paul. Yet, many preachers claim to find this truth in the Old Testament. If words have any meaning, the mystery cannot be found in the scriptures written before Paul. Therefore, we know that the Body of Christ is not the subject of what transpires in Acts 1-8 because those events were in accordance with what the prophets spoke about since the beginning of the world (Acts 3:21).

That the Godhead created all things, both visible and invisible (Col. 1:14-17), by Jesus Christ proves the deity of Christ.

(10) To the intent that now unto the principalities and powers in heavenly places might be known by the church the manifold wisdom of God,
(11) According to the eternal purpose which he purposed in Christ Jesus our Lord:

The mystery of the Body of Christ is a great demonstration of the wisdom of God. In this present age angels are not teaching us, but we are teaching them. The mystery was not an afterthought; it was God's eternal purpose that He planned before the world began (Eph. 1:4; 2 Tim. 1:9).

(12) In whom we have boldness and access with confidence by the faith of him.

What an amazing statement! As members of the Body of Christ we have boldness and access with confidence in the presence of God (Eph. 2:18). This stands in stark contrast with how God dealt with Gentiles in time past. We do not have this privilege because of our faith. We are justified by the faith of Christ (Gal. 2:16). We are to live by the faith of Christ (Gal. 2:20). We have access by the faith of Christ. Yes, we must place our faith in Christ (Gal. 3:26). However, our spiritual blessings are based upon what Christ accomplished by His faith.

(13) Wherefore I desire that ye faint not at my tribulations for you, which is your glory.

Christ suffered to purchase our salvation and Paul suffered to proclaim it (Col. 1:24). It was Paul, not Peter, who filled up the afflictions of Christ for the Body's sake. Peter suffered but for a different ministry. By the grace of God, Paul never fainted in all his tribulations (2 Cor. 4:15-18). He encouraged the Body of Christ not to faint at his tribulations (2 Tim. 1:8). It was for our eternal glory that Paul endured all the things he suffered (2 Tim. 2:8-10).

Chapter 8
The Main Division

When it comes to rightly dividing the word of truth, it is imperative that we first of all identify the main division in the scripture. Once we do that, the details in understanding God's word will start falling into place as we study with the main division in mind.

The main division in the Bible is between prophecy concerning Israel and the mystery of the Body of Christ. When God dispensed the mysteries of this present age through the apostle Paul, He fulfilled the word of God (Col. 1:25-26). The rest of scripture revolves around one main theme which is the burden of prophecy: The King and His Kingdom. That is why it was not until Paul wrote his last epistle by inspiration that we are told to rightly divide the word of truth. This does not mean that there are not mysteries related to prophecy (Matt. 13:10-17) or prophecy related to the mystery (2 Tim. 3:1-13).

Carefully compare the following ten points and consider the stark contrast between prophecy concerning Israel and the mystery of the Body of Christ.

The Prophetic Kingdom Program of Israel

(19) Repent ye therefore, and be converted, that your sins may be blotted out, when the times of refreshing shall come from the presence of the Lord;

Study Notes

(20) And he shall send Jesus Christ, which before was preached unto you:
(21) Whom the heaven must receive until the times of restitution of all things, which <u>God hath spoken by the mouth of all his holy prophets since the world began.</u>
(Acts 3:19-21)

1) Concerns a KINGDOM; a political ORGANIZATION (Dan. 2:44)
2) The kingdom to be established ON EARTH (Jer. 23:5; Matt. 6:10)
3) The kingdom PROPHESIED since the world began (Lk. 1:67-75)
4) Israel to be given SUPREMACY over the nations (Isa. 61:6)
5) The Gentiles blessed through Israel's RISE AND INSTRUMENTALITY (Zech. 8:23)
6) Prophecy mainly concerns NATIONS (Isa. 2:4)
7) Prophecy concerns blessings, both MATERIAL and spiritual, on EARTH (Isa. 11:1-9)
8) Christ comes to His people, ISRAEL, ON EARTH (Joel 3:15-17)
9) Justification is by a man's faith, and it must be a faith that WORKS (Jam. 2:24)
10) The proclamation of the prophetic program committed particularly to the TWELVE apostles (Matt. 19:28; Acts 1:6-8)

The Mystery Program of the Body of Christ

(25) Now to him that is of power to stablish you according to my gospel, and the preaching of Jesus Christ, according to <u>the revelation of the mystery, which was kept secret since the world began,</u>
(26) But now is made manifest, and by the scriptures of the prophets, according to the commandment of the everlasting God, made known to all nations for the obedience of faith: (Rom. 16:25-26)

1) Concerns a BODY; a spiritual ORGANISM (1 Cor. 12:12-13)
2) The Body is given a position in HEAVENLY places (Eph. 2:5-6)
3) The Body was chosen in Christ before the world began but kept SECRET since the world began (Eph. 1:4; 3:9)
4) Jew and Gentile placed on the SAME LEVEL before God (Rom. 10:12; 11:32), baptized into ONE body (Gal. 3:27-28)
5) The Gentiles blessed through Israel's FALL AND DIMINISHING (Rom. 11:11-12, 15)
6) The mystery concerns INDIVIDUALS (2 Cor. 5:17)
7) The mystery concerns all SPIRITUAL blessings in HEAVENLY places (Eph. 1:3)
8) Christ comes for His Body, the Church, meeting them IN THE AIR (1 Thess. 4:17)
9) Justification is by the faith of Christ (Gal. 2:16) and is received through faith WITHOUT WORKS (Rom. 3:28; 4:5)
10) The proclamation of the mystery committed particularly to PAUL (Col. 1:24-27)

The Mystery is a Parenthetical Interruption of Prophecy

(24) Seventy weeks are determined upon thy people and upon thy holy city, to finish the transgression, and to make an end of sins, and to make reconciliation for iniquity, and to bring in everlasting righteousness, and to seal up the vision and prophecy, and to anoint the most Holy.
(25) Know therefore and understand, that from the going forth of the commandment to restore and to build Jerusalem unto the Messiah the Prince shall be seven weeks, and threescore and two weeks: the street shall be built again, and the wall, even in troublous times.
(26) And after threescore and two weeks shall Messiah be cut off, but not for himself: and the people of the prince that shall come shall destroy the city and the sanctuary; and the end thereof shall be with a flood, and unto the end of the war desolations are determined.
(27) And he shall confirm the covenant with many for one week: and in the midst of the week he shall cause the sacrifice and the oblation to cease, and for the overspreading of abominations he shall make it desolate, even until the consummation, and that determined shall be poured upon the desolate. (Dan. 9:24-27)

This time schedule given to Daniel is a major key in understanding prophecy. It reveals that there are seventy weeks of years (70 x 7 = 490 years) determined upon Israel and the city of Jerusalem until Christ comes to establish His kingdom. It began with the decree to restore and build Jerusalem (Neh. 2), and sixty-nine of the weeks (483 years) were fulfilled at the time of the crucifixion of Christ. There is still one week (7 years) that is yet to be fulfilled. We commonly refer to it as the tribulation period.

We are living in a parenthetical mystery age revealed through the apostle Paul (Col. 1:24-27) in which God is building the spiritual Body of Christ. The mystery of this age interrupted the prophetic calendar of Israel, and it cannot resume until this age ends with the rapture of the Body of Christ. This explains why the final week in Daniel's prophecy has yet to be fulfilled and is separated from the sixty-ninth week by a period of about two thousand years.

The seventieth week is divided into two periods of forty-two months (3 ½ years) each (e.g., Rev. 11:2; 13:5). In the first forty-two months years the Antichrist rises to power through false peace, makes a covenant with Israel, and helps to restore the sacrificial system in the temple. But peace will be taken from the earth and wars will abound followed by famine and pestilence. In the midst of the week Satan enters the antichrist and he will break the covenant with Israel, cause the sacrifices to cease, and will sit in the temple and declare himself to be God which is "the abomination of desolation" (Matt. 24:15). This marks the beginning of the "great tribulation" which will last forty-two months. The world will be required to worship the Antichrist and those that do will receive his mark in their forehead or in their right hand. Those that refuse to take his mark and worship him will not be able to buy or sell (Rev. 13:15-18). The godly remnant of Israel that refuses to worship the beast will be the special object of his persecution. Many of them will be beheaded and the rest will flee into the wilderness where God will supernaturally provide for them just as He did in the Exodus

(Rev. 12:14). Jesus Christ said of that time, "except those days should be shortened, there shall no flesh be saved" (Matt. 24:22).

After the great tribulation, the sign of the Son of man will appear in heaven and He will return in power and great glory to destroy His enemies, save His people, and establish His kingdom. In His Olivet Discourse (Matt. 24-25), Christ prepared His apostles for the tribulation period because the mystery of this present age was yet to be revealed.

70th Week	Matthew 24	Revelation 6
"Beginning of Sorrows"	False Christs (vv.4-5)	False Christ (vv.1-2)
	Wars (vv.6-7)	Wars (vv.3-4)
	Famines (v.7)	Famine (vv.5-6)
	Pestilences, Beasts (v.7)	Pestilence, Beasts (vv.7-8)
"Great Tribulation"	Martyrs (vv.9-28)	Martyrs (vv.9-11)
"After the Tribulation"	Signs in Heaven (vv.29-30)	Signs in Heaven (vv.12-17)

The seventieth week of Daniel is the subject of much prophecy because it is the period of time that leads up to the second coming of Christ. Hebrews through Revelation, although written before Paul wrote his last epistle, are placed after his epistles because they concern resumption of the prophetic calendar of Israel. The books of the NT are not arranged chronologically, but dispensationally. The writers of the Hebrew epistles were trained in the prophetic kingdom program of Israel, which explains why the Body of Christ and its corresponding mysteries revealed through Paul are not even mentioned in those books.

Chapter 9
The Twofold Purpose of God

The main division in the word of God reveals a twofold purpose of God. Perhaps a better way to say it is that God has one great purpose that will be fulfilled through a twofold plan for the ages.

God's one great purpose is to be glorified through the Lord Jesus Christ. The twofold plan through which He will accomplish this is implied in the very first verse of the Bible. God will be glorified in heaven and earth (Gen. 1:1). As "the most high God," the Lord is the "possessor of heaven and earth" (Gen. 14:19, 22). There has been a rebellion in both heaven (beginning with Lucifer) and earth (beginning with Adam).

The twofold plan concerns how God will reconcile the governments of both heaven and earth back to Himself. Israel is His agent to reconcile the government on the earth while the Body of Christ is His agent to reconcile the government in heavenly places.

(16) For by him were all things created, that are in heaven, and that are in earth, visible and invisible, whether *they be* thrones, or dominions, or principalities, or powers: all things were created by him, and for him:
(17) And he is before all things, and by him all things consist.

(18) And he is the head of the body, the church: who is the beginning, the firstborn from the dead; that in all *things* he might have the preeminence.
(19) For it pleased *the Father* that in him should all fulness dwell;
(20) And, having made peace through the blood of his cross, by him to reconcile all things unto himself; by him, *I say,* whether *they be* things in earth, or things in heaven. (Col. 1:16-20)

Before the World Began

The rebellion against God's government began before He created Adam (Isa. 14:12-15; Ezek. 28:11-19). The creation of man was in response to Lucifer's challenge and rebellion. Please read Psalm 8 which concerns the creation of man and note especially the words, "because of thine enemies, that thou mightest still the enemy and the avenger" (v.2).

Satan and the angels that followed him operate primarily in the heavens (Eph. 2:2; 6:12; Rev. 12:8). The heavens are not clean in God's sight (Job 15:15), which is why darkness, and the firmament of heaven are the only things that God did not say were "good" in Genesis 1. When God created Adam, He commissioned him to "subdue" the earth (Gen. 1:28) which means to conquer. He said that before the fall, so we know that He was not referring to subduing wild plants and animals. Therefore, there must have been enemies already in existence.

And the earth was without form, and void; and darkness was upon the face of the deep. And the Spirit of God moved upon the face of the waters. (Gen. 1:2)

This verse describes God's judgment that came as a result of the fall of Lucifer. The only other reference to the earth being "without form and void" concerns a future judgment (Jer. 4:23), so why wouldn't the same language describe a past judgment? The opponents of this view call it "the Gap Theory" and claim that we are trying to accommodate evolution, but we reject the theory of evolution. The issue is not the duration of the gap, but the fact there was a rebellion and judgment before the world of mankind began.

From the beginning of the Bible until the ministry of Paul, God's revelation concerned His purpose for reconciling the earth, and so that was Satan's focus. In having Christ crucified, Satan thought that he had defeated or at least hindered that purpose. What he did not know was that "by the cross" (Eph. 2:16) God would form a new group of believers to give us the high privilege of reigning with Him in the heavenly places. We will occupy the thrones and principalities left vacant by Satan and his angels after they are finally cast out of heaven. This was God's purpose ever since the rebellion of Lucifer that took place BEFORE the foundation of the world, but He had to keep it a secret until Satan deceived himself by crucifying Christ.

(6) Howbeit we speak wisdom among them that are perfect: yet not the wisdom of this world, nor of the princes of this world, that come to nought:
(7) But we speak the wisdom of God in a mystery, *even* the hidden *wisdom*, which God ordained before the world unto our glory:
(8) Which none of the princes of this world knew: for had they known *it*, they would not have crucified the Lord of glory. (1 Cor. 2:6-8)

God's Purpose for the Earth Concerns the Nation of Israel

(24) The LORD of hosts hath sworn, saying, Surely as I have thought, so shall it come to pass; and as <u>I have purposed</u>, *so* shall it stand:
(25) That I will break the Assyrian in my land, and upon my mountains tread him under foot: then shall his yoke depart from off them, and his burden depart from off their shoulders.
(26) <u>This *is* the purpose that is purposed upon the whole earth</u>: and this *is* the hand that is stretched out upon all the nations.
(27) For <u>the LORD of hosts hath purposed</u>, and who shall disannul *it?* and his hand *is* stretched out, and who shall turn it back? (Isa. 14:24-27)

Upon the fall of man, God declared that He would provide a Redeemer through the "seed of the woman" (Gen. 3:15). Satan worked to prevent the promised Seed from coming into the world (e.g., Gen. 6:1-8). By the eleventh chapter of Genesis God gave up on the Gentile world (which is explained in Romans 1:18-32) and chose Abraham. He made an everlasting covenant to make of him a great nation and to give him and his seed a special land (Gen. 12:1-3). Israel is to be a light to the other nations.

God also made an everlasting covenant with David concerning his throne and kingdom (2 Sam. 7:12-16). Christ will reign on the earth from the throne of David in Jerusalem over the whole world (Ex. 19:5-6; Jer. 23:5-6). Israel will reign with Christ on earth over the nations. The kingdom was prepared FROM the foundation of the world (Matt. 25:34) and spoken by the prophets since the world began (Acts 3:21).

God's Purpose for Heaven Concerns the Body of Christ

That the Body of Christ is God's heavenly people is clear in the following references.

And hath raised us up together, and made us sit together in heavenly places in Christ Jesus: (Eph. 2:6)

For our conversation is in heaven; from whence also we look for the Saviour, the Lord Jesus Christ: (Phil. 3:20)

(1) If ye then be risen with Christ, seek those things which are above, where Christ sitteth on the right hand of God.
(2) Set your affection on things above, not on things on the earth.
(3) For ye are dead, and your life is hid with Christ in God.
(4) When Christ, *who is* our life, shall appear, then shall ye also appear with him in glory. (Col. 3:1-4)

The Body of Christ was planned BEFORE the foundation of the world (Eph. 1:4) but kept secret since the world began until it was revealed through the apostle Paul (Rom. 16:25; Eph. 3:1-13). To understand this program, we must study Paul's epistles because that is where it is revealed. We have been predestinated to be glorified with Christ and reign with Him "eternal in the heavens" (2 Cor. 5:1).

One of the spiritual blessings we have as members of the Body of Christ is that God has made known to us the mystery of His will concerning both heaven and earth.

(8) Wherein he hath abounded toward us in all wisdom and prudence;
(9) Having made known unto us the mystery of his will, according to his good pleasure which <u>he hath purposed in himself</u>:
(10) That in the dispensation of the fulness of times he might gather together in one all things in Christ, both which are in heaven, and which are on earth; *even* **in him:**
(11) In whom also we have obtained an inheritance, being predestinated according to the <u>purpose of him</u> who worketh all things after the counsel of his own will:
(12) That we should be to the praise of his glory, who first trusted in Christ. (Eph 1:8-12)

The mystery of the Body of Christ was no afterthought or "Plan B." It was God's "eternal purpose" (Eph. 3:11) that He kept hid in Himself until He revealed it through Paul. It is a demonstration of His great wisdom (Eph. 1:8; 3:10; 1 Cor. 2:7).

Those who reject dispensationalism accuse us of teaching that God failed in trying to establish His kingdom through Israel and had to come up with another plan. They claim Christ came to establish a spiritual kingdom and that His promises to Israel are fulfilled spiritually in the church. Those that "spiritualize" the plain words of scripture tell *spiritual lies.* Israel failed, not God. He knew they would fall, and He planned that through their fall He would reconcile the world to Himself (Rom. 11:11-15, 32-36).

The "dispensation of the fulness of times" is the eternal state after the creation of a new heaven and earth when the full purpose of what God revealed in time finally comes to fruition. This verse (Eph. 1:10) summarizes the goal of God's twofold purpose. Christ is central in all that God is doing. There is one family of God (Eph. 3:14-15), but there will be a distinction throughout eternity between the things in heaven and earth.

Notice in Ephesians 1:10 that the things in heaven and earth will all be gathered together "in Christ." All who are redeemed by the blood of Christ are "in Christ." A person can only be "in Adam" or "in Christ" (1 Cor. 15:22). Christ is the foundation and center of both the prophetic program (1 Pet. 2:6) and the mystery program (Eph. 2:20). So, the fact people were in Christ before Paul (Rom. 16:7) does not prove the Body of Christ began before his ministry. What makes the Body of Christ distinct is that it is a new creature (2 Cor. 5:17) that is neither Jew nor Gentile (Gal. 3:28).

Chapter 10
The Twofold Ministry of Christ

The Lord Jesus Christ is foundational and central to all that God does, but there is a difference between His earthly ministry to Israel and His heavenly ministry through Paul to the Gentiles.

Now I say that <u>Jesus Christ was a minister of the circumcision</u> for the truth of God, to confirm the promises *made* unto the fathers: (Rom. 15:8)

<u>That I should be the minister of Jesus Christ to the Gentiles</u>, ministering the gospel of God, that the offering up of the Gentiles might be acceptable, being sanctified by the Holy Ghost. (Rom. 15:16)

The earthly ministry of Christ was one of CONFIRMATION, to confirm what was already promised to the Jewish fathers, and not INAUGURATION, to reveal His secret purpose to build a new creature. Israel is God's earthly people, and He promised them a land and worldwide kingdom over the nations. Christ plainly said that He was "not sent but unto the lost sheep of the house of Israel" (Matt. 15:24). It was not that He did not care about the Gentiles, but that according to His prophetic plan the Gentiles were to be blessed through Israel's rise and glory.

In this present age, as revealed through Paul's ministry, the Gentiles are blessed through the fall and diminishing of Israel (Rom. 11:12), and believing Jews and Gentiles are baptized by one Spirit into one spiritual Body wherein there are no earthly distinctions (Gal. 3:27-28). Paul's ministry was actually the ministry of Christ from heaven and concerns things that were kept secret since the world began (Rom. 16:25; Col. 1:21-29). God used him to write thirteen epistles by inspiration to the Body of Christ. These epistles are "wholesome words, even the words of our Lord Jesus Christ" (1 Tim. 6:3). He wrote "commandments of the Lord" (1 Cor. 14:37), for Christ was speaking through him (2 Cor. 13:3).

Earthly Ministry	Heavenly Ministry
Prophecy (Lk. 24:27, 44)	Mystery (Rom. 16:25)
Confirmation (Rom. 15:8)	Inauguration (Acts 26:16)
Primary Scriptures – The Four Gospels	Exclusive Scriptures – Paul's Epistles
Christ is the King of Israel (Jn. 1:49)	Christ is the Head of One Body (2 Cor. 5:16-17)
Dispensation of Law (Matt. 5:17-20; 23:1-3)	Dispensation of Grace (Rom. 6:14; Eph. 3:1-13)
Gospel of the Kingdom (Matt. 4:23)	Gospel of the Grace of God (Acts 20:24)
Difference Jew and Gentile (Matt. 15:21-28)	No Difference Jew and Gentile (Gal. 3:27-28)
Sent 12 to Israel (Matt. 10:5-6)	Sent Paul to the Gentiles (Rom. 11:13)
Signs Abound (Jn. 20:30-31)	Signs Ceased (1 Cor. 13:8-13)
Kingdom Commission (Mk. 16:15-18)	Grace Commission (2 Cor. 5:18-20)
Second Coming (Matt. 24:29-31)	Secret Coming (1 Cor. 15:51-52)

Chapter 11
The Twofold People of God

One of the fundamental tenets of rightly dividing the word of truth is understanding and maintaining the difference between Israel and the Church which is the Body of Christ. The main division in the Bible (prophecy vs. mystery), the twofold purpose of God (heaven and earth), and the twofold ministry of Christ (earthly and heavenly) clearly prove this difference. In this chapter we are going to take a basic overview of Israel and the Body of Christ. By comparing their purpose, origin, program, and destiny we will see how different they are.

Israel

1) The Purpose of Israel

Israel is God's agent to establish His kingdom on the earth (Ex. 19:5-6). The nations will come to worship God through their ministry (Isa. 2:1-5; Matt. 28:19-20). God spoke about this purpose through His prophets since the world began (Lk. 1:70; Acts 3:21).

2) The Origin of Israel

When Adam fell, he lost his dominion on the earth. God immediately promised a Saviour who would redeem what Adam ruined (Gen. 3:15). As God progressively revealed His plan, it became more and more specific: He would come through Seth,

Noah, Shem, Abraham, Isaac, Jacob, Judah, David, and ultimately a virgin (Isa. 7:14). Abraham is the father of the Hebrew people (Gen. 14:13). There are a number of passages in the Bible that review Israel's history and they all begin with Abraham.

God only used eleven chapters to cover the first two thousand years of human history (Genesis 1-11) but thirty-nine books (Genesis 12 - Malachi) to cover the next sixteen hundred years. He used just two chapters in Genesis to tell us about creation, but the next thirty-nine chapters to tell us all about Abraham, Isaac, and Jacob. The books of Exodus through Malachi are all about the nation that sprang forth from Abraham. The children of Israel became a nation when God redeemed them out of Egypt. Gentiles are only dealt with in their relation to Israel.

In Romans 1:18-32 we find the divine commentary on the history of mankind leading up to the call of Abraham. God "gave them up" (the Gentile world) at the tower of Babel. In light of the events of Genesis 1-11, the covenant that God made with Abraham sets forth God's plan and purpose for using a nation of His own creation to reconcile the earth back to Himself (Gen. 12:1-3).

3) The Program of Israel

God deals with Israel by covenants. The covenants do not pertain to the Body of Christ (Rom. 9:1-5; Eph. 2:11-13). A covenant is an agreement or promise (Isa. 28:14-18). God's covenants with man originate with Him and are given in relation to the earth. Some are conditional while others are unconditional. Some are temporal while others are everlasting.

Israel's Covenants:
1) Abrahamic (Gen. 12:1-3; 15:18) – everlasting
2) Law (Ex. 24:3-8; 34:27-28) – temporary
3) Land (Deut. 29:1) – temporary
4) Davidic (2 Sam. 7:12-17; 23:1-5) – everlasting
5) New (Jer. 31:31-34; Heb. 8:7-13) – everlasting

The covenants build upon each other, the Abrahamic Covenant is foundational to the others.

4) The Destiny of Israel

Israel failed. They rejected the Father throughout the Old Testament, the Son of God in the Gospels, and the Holy Ghost in the book of Acts. They fell when they stoned Stephen (Acts 7:54-60; Rom. 11:11-15). They were diminished through a transition period that is recorded in the book of Acts. They are now set aside as a nation in judicial blindness.

Individual Jews can still be saved in this age, but they are saved the same way as Gentiles and baptized into one Body wherein there is neither Jew nor Gentile (Gal. 3:27-28).

After this age ends with the rapture, God will resume His dealings with Israel and fulfill all the prophecies and promises concerning them. The Body of Christ did not replace Israel and is not spiritual Israel (Jer. 31:35-37; Rom. 11:25-29).

The Body of Christ

1) The Purpose of the Body of Christ

The Body of Christ is God's heavenly people (Eph. 2:6-7; Phil. 3:20-21; Col. 3:1-4). God purposed to build the spiritual Body of Christ before the foundation of the world, but He kept it secret since the world began until He revealed it to the apostle Paul (Rom. 16:25; Eph. 3:1-13). The nation of Israel is God's agent to reconcile the government of earth to Himself, but the Body of Christ is His agent to reconcile the heavens (Col. 1:16-20).

2) The Origin of the Body of Christ

There are many views concerning the historical beginning of the Body of Christ. This is an important issue because it has major doctrinal ramifications. It should be obvious that it did not begin before the resurrection and ascension of Christ, otherwise it would be a Headless Body (Eph. 1:20-22).

The most popular view is that the Day of Pentecost in Acts 2 was the birthday of the church. It is assumed that when the Holy Ghost was poured out on that day, He began to form the spiritual Body of Christ. However, there are many problems with that view.

    1. The church in Acts 2 existed before Pentecost.

A church is simply a called-out assembly. During the earthly ministry of Christ there was a "little flock" of believing Jews that were called out of unbelieving Israel (Lk. 12:32). The three thousand Jews that repented and were baptized were ADDED to that church (Acts 2:41, 47). How could they be added to a church that did not already exist? Therefore, Acts 2 does not record the birthday of any church. It does record how Christ empowered His disciples by pouring out the Holy Ghost upon them, and how three thousand Jews repented from killing their Messiah and were added to that holy nation (Matt. 21:43; 1 Pet. 2:9).

    2. What happened in Acts 2 was according to PROPHECY (Acts 2:16-17; 3:24).

The Body of Christ was a mystery which "was kept SECRET since the world began" (Rom. 16:25). The prophesied "last days" of Israel could not be at the same time the first days of the Body of Christ. The Body of Christ was a mystery hid from the prophets (Eph. 3:1-12).

    3. Pentecost was a Jewish feast day.

Pentecost was one of the three annual feasts at which every male was required to appear at the sanctuary in Jerusalem (Ex. 23:14-17). The seven annual feasts that God gave to Israel (see Lev. 23) provide a prophetic picture concerning His dealings with them. On the day after the seventh Sabbath (50 days, *pente* = 50) was a celebration of the anticipated harvest. On this day two wave loafs with leaven were offered before the Lord. Some say these two loaves picture Jews and Gentiles that were baptized into one Body in Acts 2. However, the only Gentiles present in Acts 2 were proselytes to Judaism (v.10). There were NO uncircumcised Gentiles present or even welcome. Also, the Body of Christ is not pictured by two loaves but ONE BREAD (1 Cor. 10:17). The loaves picture the division of Israel and Judah that will be made one in the kingdom (Ezek. 37:16-23). God appointed the day of Pentecost as the day He would begin to pour out His Spirit. This was the baptism with the Holy Ghost that the Father promised and was in anticipation of the Kingdom Age. There will be Gentiles in the kingdom (Matt. 25:31-46), but they will not be in one spiritual Body with Israel.

4. The kingdom was reoffered to Israel in the early chapters of Acts (3:19-21).

God did not begin to reconcile both believing Jews and Gentiles into one Body until after the fall of Israel (Rom. 11:11-15).

5. Peter did not preach the gospel of the grace of God in Acts 2.

The gospel of the kingdom required repentance and water baptism for the remission of sins (Mk. 1:4; Acts 2:36-40), and it was accompanied by signs of the kingdom. Peter was not preaching the same gospel that Paul received by revelation of Jesus Christ (Gal. 1:11-12; 1 Cor. 15:1-4). It is believing the gospel of the grace of God that puts us in the Body of Christ (Eph. 3:6). Peter preached the cross, but he preached it as BAD news. He preached the cross as a murder indictment on Israel as he called on them to repent for killing their Messiah.

6. The baptism "with the Holy Ghost" (Acts 1:4-5) is NOT what forms the Body of Christ.

There are many different baptisms in the Bible. There are two different baptisms that involve the Holy Spirit.

With the Holy Ghost	**By the Spirit**
Prophecy (Isa. 32:15)	Mystery (Col. 1:24-27)
Christ is the Baptizer (Matt. 3:11)	The Spirit is the Baptizer (1 Cor. 12:13)
For Power (Lk. 24:49)	For Salvation (Gal. 3:26-28)
Signs (Acts 2:4)	No Signs (Rom. 6:3)

The modern versions hide this distinction by referring to both as the baptism "in the Spirit" (cf. Acts 1:5; 1 Cor. 12:13).

7. In the early chapters of Acts, the manner in which the disciples were living was a foretaste of the kingdom they were preaching (Heb. 6:5).

Christ required His disciples to sell all that they had and give it to the poor (Lk. 12:32-33). This proved that they believed the kingdom was at hand. Since the kingdom was about to be set up, they did not need houses and lands (Acts 2:42-45; 4:32-35). The Body of Christ is instructed by Paul to do our own work that we might not lack, and to provide for our own house (1 Thess. 4:11-12; 1 Tim. 5:8). That is certainly different than selling our possessions and having all things common.

The church in Acts 2 was a prophesied Jewish church (Ps. 22:22; Heb. 2:12; Matt. 16:18) that was looking for the kingdom to be established on the earth. Everything that happened in Acts 2 was in line with prophecy concerning Israel (Acts 2:16). Peter, filled with the Holy Ghost, preached to Israel, calling on the nation to repent for killing their Messiah. The apostles were baptized with the Holy Ghost and did the signs and wonders of the kingdom they were preaching ("powers of the world to come," Heb. 6:5).

If we know how a person gets into the Body of Christ, we can know when it began historically. We are made members of the Body of Christ "by the gospel" (Eph. 3:6). Which gospel? We are baptized by one Spirit into one Body when we believe the gospel that Christ revealed first to Paul (1 Cor. 15:1-4; Gal. 1:11-12).

The Body of Christ is made up of all believers in this present age of grace. It is neither Jew nor Gentile, but one new spiritual man (Gal. 3:27-28). All who are in the Body of Christ are in Christ, but not all who are in Christ are in the Body of Christ. Israel will be "in Christ" when they are saved under the new covenant (e.g., Isa. 45:17). In the eternal state, all things will be gathered together in Christ (Eph. 1:10), but there will still be a distinction between Israel and the Body of Christ.

The age of grace began with a glorious appearing when the message of grace came down (Acts 9:1-9; Titus 2:11), and it will end with a glorious appearing when those who believed that message will be caught up to meet the Lord in the air (1 Thess. 4:17; Titus 2:13). It seems clear that Paul taught that this present age of grace began with his salvation and ministry (1 Cor. 3:10-11; 1 Tim. 1:12-16). A dispensation cannot begin before the revelations that make it a distinct dispensation are dispensed!

3) The Program of the Body of Christ

God deals with Israel according to covenants, but He deals with us under grace (Rom. 6:14-15). Of course, God showed grace in His dealings with Israel, but there is a difference between grace in a dispensation and a dispensation of grace.

Law vs. Grace

Most believers today would be surprised to learn what the apostle Paul taught concerning our relation to the law. Most churches are legalistic because they do not recognize, nor follow, Paul as the divinely appointed pattern and spokesman for the Body of Christ. The Pauline epistles are the most neglected books of the Bible in the average church today.

The book of Romans is the foundational book of doctrine for this age of grace. In Romans, Paul systematically lays out the wonderful truth that we are justified and sanctified by faith without the deeds of the law. Paul wrote Galatians to correct the legalism that was creeping into the churches of Galatia and shows plainly that we cannot mix law and grace. We are saved by grace, and we are to live our Christin life under grace. All religious denominations teach that you must do certain works to either be saved and/or to stay right with God.

In Romans and Galatians, the apostle Paul plainly states that:
- We are not justified by the law (Rom. 3:19-28; Gal. 2:16).
- We are not under the law in our walk (Rom. 6:14; Gal. 5:18).
- We are dead to the law (Rom. 7:1-4; Gal. 2:19).
- We are delivered from the law (Rom. 7:5-6; Gal. 5:1).

That we are not under the law but under grace is dispensational truth because it has not always been that way. In time past, Israel was under the law. But now, in this present age, the Body of Christ is under grace. There was nothing wrong with the law, but it was an inferior system because of the weakness of the flesh (Rom. 7:7-14; 8:1-4). God has shown grace in every age, but this is the age of grace in which He is showing grace to a greater degree than ever (Rom. 5:20-21; 1 Tim. 1:14). We have a glorious standing in grace (Rom. 5:1-2). We are complete in Christ (Col. 2:10). We are accepted in the beloved (Eph. 1:6). We cannot earn God's favor and blessings; we have it as a free gift through Jesus Christ.

What is the fundamental difference between law and grace? It is the difference between performance and a gift (cf. Ex. 19:5-6; Lk. 10:25-28 with Eph. 2:8-10; Titus 2:11-14). The law said do and be blessed, but grace says you are blessed, now go do (Deut. 28:1-5; Eph. 1:3). The law required righteousness, but grace makes us righteous. The law gave works for man to do, but grace gave words for man to believe. The law cursed sinners, but grace justifies them. The law was the ministration of death, but grace gives life. The law is about religion, but grace is about relationship.

4) The Destiny of the Body of Christ

The Body of Christ is predestinated to be glorified with Christ and reign with Him in heavenly places (Rom. 8:28-30; 2 Cor. 5:1; Eph. 2:6-7; 2 Tim. 4:18). Our rapture is imminent (Rom. 13:11-12; Phil. 4:5). We must be caught up to meet the Lord in the air before the seventieth week of Daniel can begin. In 2 Thessalonians 2, the "what" in verse 6 refers to this present age and the "he" in verse 7 refers to the Body of Christ.

(6) And now ye know what withholdeth that he might be revealed in his time.
(7) For the mystery of iniquity doth already work: only he who now letteth will let, until he be taken out of the way.

Chapter 12
The Book Between

If the book of Acts were not in the Bible, it would be confusing to read the epistles of Paul immediately after the Gospel records. We would wonder, "Who is Paul?" and "Why does he teach some things differently from what Jesus Christ taught in His earthly ministry?"

The book of Acts is the historical record of the transition period between the prophetic kingdom program of Israel and the mystery program of the Body of Christ.

By comparing Acts 1:1-2 with Luke 1:1-4, it is clear that God used Luke to write the book of Acts. He wrote sometime after Paul's earliest ministry in Rome because that is where its history ends in chapter 28 (early 60's AD). Luke was with Paul until his death (2 Tim. 4:11) and we know Paul's ministry continued after Acts 28. So why did Luke stop the record where he did? Because the book of Acts is the record of the fall and diminishing of Israel. God set His chosen nation aside through a transition as He called out a believing remnant from among them. Acts concludes with the end of that transition.

The Gospel of Luke records "all that Jesus BEGAN both to do and teach, until the day in which he was taken up." The book of Acts takes up the history where the Gospel of Luke left off and records what Jesus CONTINUED to do from Heaven through the Holy Ghost sent down to empower the apostles.

By comparing how the Gospel of Luke concluded (Lk. 24:36-53) with how the book of Acts opens (Acts 1:1-12), it is easy to see that Acts is the sequel to Luke. Therefore, the same kingdom program of Israel recorded in the Gospels continues into the book of Acts.

The message to Israel in the Gospels was "repent, for the kingdom of heaven is at hand" (Matt. 3:2; 4:17; 10:5-7). The kingdom of heaven is the literal and visible kingdom that the God of heaven will establish on the earth (Dan. 2:44). Christ will rule from the throne of David in Jerusalem (Acts 2:30) and Israel will be a kingdom of priests with authority over the nations (Ex. 19:5-6; 1 Pet. 2:9).

Christ "came unto his own, and his own received him not" (Jn. 1:11). The Jews rejected their King and crucified Him. Many believe and teach that God set Israel aside at the time of the cross and immediately began this present dispensation. However, consider what Jesus prayed from the cross.

Then said Jesus, Father, forgive them; for they know not what they do. (Lk. 23:34a)

Both Christ and Peter (Acts 3:17) said that the Jews crucified their King in ignorance and therefore they are given an opportunity to repent. If we are going to understand the book of Acts, we must understand that it records a renewed offer of the kingdom to the nation of Israel.

(17) And now, brethren, I wot that through ignorance ye did it, as did also your rulers.

(18) But those things, which God before had shewed by the mouth of all his prophets, that Christ should suffer, he hath so fulfilled.
(19) Repent ye therefore, and be converted, that your sins may be blotted out, when the times of refreshing shall come from the presence of the Lord;
(20) And he shall send Jesus Christ, which before was preached unto you:
(21) Whom the heaven must receive until the times of restitution of all things, which God hath spoken by the mouth of all his holy prophets since the world began. (Acts 3:17-21)

In Romans 11:11-12, the apostle Paul speaks of the fall of Israel. When did Israel fall as a nation? When they blasphemed the Holy Ghost (Matt. 12:31-32) by stoning Stephen. They rejected the Father throughout the Old Testament. They rejected the Son of God in the Gospel records. They rejected the Holy Ghost in the early chapters of Acts. Three strikes and you are out!

**(54) When they heard these things, they were cut to the heart, and they gnashed on him with *their* teeth.
(55) But he, being full of the Holy Ghost, looked up stedfastly into heaven, and saw the glory of God, and Jesus standing on the right hand of God,
(56) And said, Behold, I see the heavens opened, and the Son of man standing on the right hand of God.
(57) Then they cried out with a loud voice, and stopped their ears, and ran upon him with one accord,
(58) And cast *him* out of the city, and stoned *him:* and the witnesses laid down their clothes at a young man's feet, whose name was Saul.** (Acts 7:54-58)

The remainder of the book of Acts (chapters 8-28) records the "diminishing" of Israel (Rom. 11:12) through a transition period. Therefore, the bulk of the books is a historical record of God moving from Israel to the Body of Christ; from the gospel of the kingdom to the gospel of the grace of God; from the ministry of Peter (1-12) to that of Paul (13-28).

The traditional view of Acts is that from beginning to end it is primarily the record of the birth and growth of the church in this present age. We are told that it contains the doctrines and practices of the church in its purest form and therefore we should seek to follow it as the pattern for ministry today. If you sincerely try to do that, you will run into some major problems.

- Which message should we preach to those who want to know how to be saved, Acts 2:37-38 or 16:30-31?
- Where and to whom should we preach? Should we, like the 12, begin at Jerusalem (Acts 1:8)? Or should we, like Paul, depart from Jerusalem and go far hence to the Gentiles (Acts 22:21)?
- Should we preach to the Jews only (Acts 11:19), to the Jews first and then the Gentiles (Acts 18:6), or to everybody alike?
- Do we receive the Holy Ghost several years after repentance and baptism (Acts 2:4), immediately after repentance and baptism (Acts 2:38), after the apostles from Jerusalem lay hands on us (Acts 8:14-17), or before baptism (Acts 10:44-48)?
- How are we to handle money? Should we sell all our possessions and have all things common with the church (Acts 2:44-45; 4:32-35) or should we work to supply for our needs (Acts 20:33-34)?

- Should we expect miraculous deliverance such as Peter's release from prison (Acts 12:7) or imprisonment in chains with Paul (Acts 26:27)?

Trying to use the whole book of Acts as a basis for doctrine today is dangerous. This transitional book is like a bridge that takes us from one dispensation to another. If you park on a bridge, you will get run over! Even in Paul's ministry there were some things he did during the transition as he worked to get a remnant out of Israel before they were officially set aside as a nation (Rom. 11:1-15; 1 Cor. 9:19-23) that we do not do today. For example, Paul participated in Jewish vows and feasts, but he never did such things because he thought they were necessary, but only because he was trying to reach the Jews.

The correct view of Acts is that from beginning to end it is primarily the account of the fall and diminishing of Israel. It explains step by step why the chosen people had to be set aside, and salvation sent to the Gentiles apart from them (Acts 13:46; 18:6; 28:28). It reveals why the commission of the twelve apostles had to be suspended and another apostle raised up to go to the Gentiles with the gospel of the grace of God.

Chapter 13
Things that Differ

The whole Bible is good because it is the word of truth, but some things are more excellent for us in this present age of grace.

(9) And this I pray, that your love may abound yet more and more in knowledge and *in* all judgment;
(10) That ye may approve things that are excellent; that ye may be sincere and without offence till the day of Christ;
(11) Being filled with the fruits of righteousness, which are by Jesus Christ, unto the glory and praise of God. (Phil. 1:9-11)

The law God revealed through Moses for Israel was more excellent than what all of the other nations lived by (Ps. 147:19-20; Rom. 2:17-20). However, under grace, we have something more excellent than what Israel had under the law (Phil. 3:1-11).

If we fail to see the things that differ in the Bible, we will not be able to discern the things that are excellent for the Body of Christ in this present age.

There are Different Gospels in the Bible

The traditional view that there is only one gospel message in the whole Bible is false. There is only one gospel by which sinners are saved today, but there is certainly more than one message of good news from God in the Bible. The word "gospel" means good tidings from God (cf. Isa. 61:1 with Lk. 4:18). We simply need to compare the content of the various gospels to see that there are different messages of good news in different ages.

The easiest way to prove there are different gospels in the Bible is by comparing the following two passages.

(31) Then he took *unto him* the twelve, and said unto them, Behold, we go up to Jerusalem, and all things that are written by the prophets concerning the Son of man shall be accomplished.
(32) For he shall be delivered unto the Gentiles, and shall be mocked, and spitefully entreated, and spitted on:
(33) And they shall scourge *him,* and put him to death: and the third day he shall rise again.
(34) And they understood none of these things: and this saying was hid from them, neither knew they the things which were spoken. (Lk. 18:31-34)

(1) Moreover, brethren, I declare unto you the gospel which I preached unto you, which also ye have received, and wherein ye stand;
(2) By which also ye are saved, if ye keep in memory what I preached unto you, unless ye have believed in vain.
(3) For I delivered unto you first of all that which I also received, how that Christ died for our sins according to the scriptures;
(4) And that he was buried, and that he rose again the third day according to the scriptures: (1 Cor. 15:1-4)

The twelve apostles had been preaching the "gospel of the kingdom" for quite some time before Christ began to speak to them about His death, burial, and resurrection, and when He did, they did not understand what He was talking about. If there is not more than one gospel in the Bible, the apostles were lost during the earthly ministry of Christ because the gospel Paul preached was hid from them (2 Cor. 4:3). They were not lost because they believed the message that was to be preached at that time, and it was different from what Christ later revealed through Paul.

Paul said the basis of the gospel was "according to the scriptures" because the facts of the death and resurrection of Christ were prophesied, but what all it accomplished was not known until Christ revealed it first to him (Gal. 1:11-12). That is why Paul is the first one in the Bible to glory in the cross and preach it as good news (Gal. 6:14).

The gospel of the kingdom, which was the good news that the prophesied kingdom promised to Israel was at hand, required water baptism as an expression of repentance and faith (Matt. 24:14; Mk. 16:15-18; Acts 2:38), but Paul plainly said that Christ sent him not to baptize but to preach the gospel (1 Cor. 1:17).

Through Paul's ministry, the gospel was preached "in all the world" and "to every creature" in the first century (Col. 1:6, 23). This proves that the gospel of the grace of God and the gospel of the kingdom are different messages, otherwise, you have Christ making a mistake in His Olivet Discourse because He said that the end would come when the gospel of the kingdom had been preached in "all the world."

(14) And this gospel of the kingdom shall be preached in all the world for a witness unto all nations; and then shall the end come. (Matt. 24:14)

There is a difference between the "gospel of the circumcision" that was committed to Peter and the "gospel of the uncircumcision" that was committed to Paul (Gal. 2:7). Many claim that this is the same message, the only distinction being to whom it was preached. If that were true, why did Paul need to communicate his gospel to the Jewish apostles if they already knew it?

(1) Then fourteen years after I went up again to Jerusalem with Barnabas, and took Titus with *me* also.
(2) And I went up by revelation, and communicated unto them that gospel which I preach among the Gentiles, but privately to them which were of reputation, lest by any means I should run, or had run, in vain. (Gal. 2:1-2)

There were gospel messages in the Old Testament. When God promised Abraham that in him all nations would be blessed, it was good news (Gal. 3:8). The book of Hebrews speaks of the gospel that was preached to Israel in the wilderness when they came up to the border of the promised land (Heb. 3:14-4:2).

God sends an angel to preach "the everlasting gospel" to those who dwell on the earth in the future tribulation period (Rev. 14:6-7). Included in that message is the announcement that the "hour of his judgment is come." How could that be the message for today when we are living in "the day of salvation" (2 Cor. 6:2)? This proves that the Body of Christ will not go through the tribulation period, otherwise, that angel of God would be accursed (Gal. 1:8).

There is only one gospel by which we are saved in this age. Preachers help Satan keep sinners in spiritual darkness (2 Cor. 4:3-4) when they preach Acts 2:38 instead of Acts 16:31.

(37) Now when they heard *this,* they were pricked in their heart, and said unto Peter and to the rest of the apostles, Men, *and* brethren what shall we do?
(38) Then Peter said unto them, Repent, and be baptized every one of you in the name of Jesus Christ for the remission of sins, and ye shall receive the gift of the Holy Ghost. (Acts 2:37-38)

(30) And brought them out, and said, Sirs, what must I do to be saved?
(31) And they said, Believe on the Lord Jesus Christ, and thou shalt be saved, and thy house. (Acts 16:30-31)

The gospel that Christ revealed through the apostle Paul is the good news that sinners can be justified freely by grace through trusting Christ and what He accomplished for us through His death, burial, and resurrection. To add any works to the finished work of Christ is to pervert the gospel.

(6) I marvel that ye are so soon removed from him that called you into the grace of Christ unto another gospel:
(7) Which is not another; but there be some that trouble you, and would pervert the gospel of Christ.

(8) But though we, or an angel from heaven, preach any other gospel unto you than that which we have preached unto you, let him be accursed.
(9) As we said before, so say I now again, If any *man* preach any other gospel unto you than that ye have received, let him be accursed.
(10) For do I now persuade men, or God? or do I seek to please men? for if I yet pleased men, I should not be the servant of Christ.
(11) But I certify you, brethren, that the gospel which was preached of me is not after man.
(12) For I neither received it of man, neither was I taught *it,* but by the revelation of Jesus Christ. (Gal. 1:6-12)

There are Different Churches in the Bible

The word "church" occurs seventy-seven times in the King James Bible and thirty-seven times in the plural for a total of a hundred and fourteen references. There is no need to look to the Greek to understand the word, for its definition is clear when you study the English word as it is used in the KJB. It is a special Bible word that refers to *an assembly called out by God* in every reference except one. Nowhere in the Bible is it used in reference to a denomination or a building.

In Acts 19, the KJB translators translated the Greek word *ekklesia* as "assembly" three times instead of "church" because it is not referring to God's church (v.32, 39, 41). In putting "assembly" instead of "church," the KJB makes a doctrinal difference between an unruly union mob and an orderly congregation of God's people. However, they translated a different Greek word, *hierosulous*, as "robbers of churches" (Acts

19:37). The modern versions say "temples" instead of "churches." The Spirit of God led the translators to put "churches" instead of "temples" in order to teach us that buildings in which people worship idols would be known as churches. There are many so-called churches today that are not really God's church because they are preaching a false gospel and teaching false doctrine. Satan has counterfeit churches (2 Cor. 11:4, 13-15).

If we study the word "church" as it used in the Bible without trying to prove any preconceived ideas, and we let the Bible say what it plainly says, as we compare scripture with scripture, we will learn that there are different churches that exist in different dispensations. The context determines which church is being referred to.

It is a great blunder to assume that the word church is used exclusively for this present age. That is why we should shy away from using the term, "Church Age." Dispensationalists such as Scofield, Larkin, Chafer, and Ryrie emphasized the difference between Israel and the Church. However, Israel was and will yet be a church.

Failure to recognize the different churches in the Bible will lead to doctrinal and practical problems. There is much bad doctrine about the church because of a failure to rightly divide the different churches in the Bible. For example, that is why some think there is only a local and visible church and that you must be water baptized to be a member of it. The Baptist Confession of Faith of 1646 states (emphasis mine): *"the church is a company of VISIBLE saints, called and separated from the world by the Word and Spirit of God, to the VISIBLE profession of the faith; being BAPTIZED into that faith"* (Article 33).

1) The Church in the Wilderness

**(37) This is that Moses, which said unto the children of Israel, A prophet shall the Lord your God raise up unto you of your brethren, like unto me; him shall ye hear.
(38) This is he, that was in the church in the wilderness with the angel which spake to him in the mount Sina, and *with* our fathers: who received the lively oracles to give unto us:** (Acts 7:37-38)

God called Israel out of Egypt, and they were assembled in the wilderness. They were baptized unto Moses (1 Cor. 10:1) and brought under the covenant of the law. They were an earthly people with earthly blessings and an earthly inheritance (Ex. 19:5-6). There was certainly a difference between Israel and the Gentiles in that church.

2) The Prophesied Kingdom Church

I will declare thy name unto my brethren: in the midst of the congregation will I praise thee. (Ps. 22:22)

Saying, I will declare thy name unto my brethren, in the midst of the church will I sing praise unto thee. (Heb. 2:12)

This cannot be the church which was a mystery hid in God (Eph. 3:9). The church in prophecy is the church Christ spoke of in His earthly ministry concerning the kingdom of heaven (Matt. 16:18-19). Israel will be called out of the nations and assembled in their land (Ezek. 11:17; 36:24-28) under the new covenant (Heb. 12:18-29).

3) The Little Flock

Fear not, little flock; for it is your Father's good pleasure to give you the kingdom. (Lk. 12:32)

There was a little flock of believing Jews in the earthly ministry of Christ that were called out of apostate Israel (Matt. 18:15-20). They were called out by believing the gospel of the kingdom. Repentance and water baptism were required to be part of that church. It was called the "church at Jerusalem" in the book of Acts. The three thousand Jews that repented on the Day of Pentecost were added to a church that already existed (Acts 2:36-47). The events of early Acts concern what was spoken by the prophets since the world began (Acts 3:21). The kingdom church was phased out through a transition after God raised up the apostle Paul.

4) The Church which is the Body of Christ

For the perfecting of the saints, for the work of the ministry, for the edifying of the body of Christ: (Eph. 4:12)

The church that God is building in this present dispensation is made up of all those who believe the gospel of the grace of God. Immediately upon salvation, we are baptized by one Spirit into one Body (1 Cor. 12:13). All believers in this present age are members of the church, which is the Body of Christ (Eph. 1:15-23). The word church is used nine times in Ephesians, and in every case, it is referring to the one true and spiritual church that God is building in this present age.

Consider some of the distinctive truths about the Body of Christ in Ephesians in contrast with Israel.

- Blessed with all spiritual blessings in heavenly places (1:3)
- Chosen in Christ before the foundation of the world (1:4)
- Heavenly calling and position (2:5-7)
- One NEW man, neither Jew nor Gentile (2:11-18)
- Mystery hid in God and first revealed to Paul (3:1-12)
- The unity of the Spirit (4:1-6)
- Christ and His Church are a great mystery (5:32)
- Spiritual warfare (6:10-20)

5) The Local Church

(3) Greet Priscilla and Aquila my helpers in Christ Jesus: (4) Who have for my life laid down their own necks: unto whom not only I give thanks, but also all the churches of the Gentiles. (5) Likewise *greet* the church that is in their house. Salute my wellbeloved Epaenetus, who is the firstfruits of Achaia unto Christ. (Rom. 16:3-5)

There is one Body of Christ but many local churches. The members of the Body of Christ should assemble together locally, if at all possible, for the work of the ministry. The local church is a visible representation of the Body of Christ in a community. The apostle Paul started local churches and wrote epistles to local churches. The local church is an assembly of believers that is organized according to the order set forth in Paul's epistles (e.g., bishops and deacons, Phil. 1:1). We must not require more from people than God does to be part of our local church. There is not one instance of the apostle Paul requiring water baptism for church membership. He does not mention water baptism in the Pastoral Epistles.

6) Future Churches in the Tribulation Period

(10) I was in the Spirit on the Lord's day, and heard behind me a great voice, as of a trumpet,
(11) Saying, I am Alpha and Omega, the first and the last: and, What thou seest, write in a book, and send *it* unto the seven churches which are in Asia; unto Ephesus, and unto Smyrna, and unto Pergamos, and unto Thyatira, and unto Sardis, and unto Philadelphia, and unto Laodicea. (Rev. 1:10-11)

The seven churches in the book of Revelation are representative churches of the tribulation saints. John was transported in the Spirit out into the future "Lord's day" to be an eyewitness of the things he wrote. The "Lord's day" is not a reference to a day of the week, but to the prophetic "day of the Lord." Therefore, the whole book of Revelation is a "prophecy" that will be fulfilled after this present age concludes with the rapture of the Body of Christ (Rev. 1:3; 22:7, 10, 18-19). The seven letters in chapters two and three deal with the problems that tribulation saints will have to overcome in order to obtain the promised blessings of the kingdom. The Body of Christ is blessed by grace according to who we are in Christ (Eph. 1:3), and not by overcoming anything.

It should be clear that the Body of Christ does not need the following promises.

He that hath an ear, let him hear what the Spirit saith unto the churches; To him that overcometh will I give to eat of the tree of life, which is in the midst of the paradise of God. (Rev. 2:7)

He that hath an ear, let him hear what the Spirit saith unto the churches; He that overcometh shall not be hurt of the second death. (Rev. 2:11)

The distinction between Jews and Gentiles will be a factor once again in the tribulation period.

I know thy works, and tribulation, and poverty, (but thou art rich) and *I know* the blasphemy of them which say they are Jews, and are not, but *are* the synagogue of Satan. (Rev. 2:9)

Behold, I will make them of the synagogue of Satan, which say they are Jews, and are not, but do lie; behold, I will make them to come and worship before thy feet, and to know that I have loved thee. (Rev. 3:9)

There are Different Judgments in the Bible

Most Bible commentaries present the idea that there is only one general judgment that will come at the end of the world. If we rightly divide the word of truth, we will find that there are four main judgments to come. They are different as to who is being judged, when they are judged, where they are judged, why they are judged, how they are judged (i.e., the basis), and what the results of the judgment will be. The common denominator is that the Lord Jesus Christ will be the Judge in all four judgments (Jn. 5:22, 27).

I. **The Judgment Seat of Christ (Rom. 14:10-12; 2 Cor. 5:9-11)**
   A. Who? The Body of Christ.
   B. When? Upon the resurrection and rapture of the Body of Christ.
   C. Where? In the air (1 Thess. 4:17)
   D. Why? Our service (not sins, all of our sins were judged on the cross).
   E. How? Faithfulness to the mysteries of God (1 Cor. 3:10-15; 4:1-5).
   F. What? Rewards in our reign with Christ in His heavenly kingdom (2 Tim. 4:8, 18)

II. **The Judgment of Israel (Jer. 30:7; Ezek. 20:33-38; Rev. 11:15-19)**
   A. Who? Israel - the first resurrection of prophecy (Rev. 20:1-6).
   B. When? During the 70th week of Daniel and upon the 2nd Coming of Christ.
   C. Where? On the earth.
   D. Why? To purge out the rebels (Ezek. 20:38) and set up the kingdom.
   E. How? Faith and works according to the kingdom program.
   F. What? Rewards in reigning with Christ on earth (Matt. 16:27).

III. The Judgment of the Nations (Matt. 25:31-46)
  A. Who? The Gentile nations.
  B. When? The second coming of Christ.
  C. Where? In the valley of Jehoshaphat (Joel 3:2).
  D. Why? To determine entrance into the kingdom.
  E. How? How the Gentiles treated the believing remnant of Israel.
  F. What? Blessing or cursing (cf. Gen. 12:3).

IV. The Great White Throne Judgment (Rev. 20:11-15)
  A. Who? The lost souls of all ages - the resurrection of damnation.
  B. When? After the millennial reign of Christ.
  C. Where? "there was found no place for them" (v.11)
  D. Why? Sin (Rev. 21:8).
  E. How? The books and their works.
  F. What? The lake of fire.

To mix these four different judgments together leads to confusion and false doctrine.

Chapter 14
More Things that Differ

There are Different Commissions in the Bible

As people begin to learn how to rightly divide the word of truth, they inevitably come to a crossroads where they must decide to keep going where the word of God is leading them or to veer off and stick with traditional teaching that the professing church is comfortable with. Those who fear man more than God prefer to be mainstream to avoid any reproach. Some people will rightly divide until it becomes inconvenient and gets them in trouble. For example, nearly all professing Christians believe that the "Great Commission" found at the end of the Gospel records and in the first chapter of Acts is the marching orders of the Church. Are you willing to reconsider this view in light of dispensational truth?

There are many commissions from God in the Bible and all of them are great because God gave them. What right do we have to elevate one above the others and call it "THE Great Commission?" We cannot obey all of them at the same time. For example, compare "Go not into the way of the Gentiles" (Matt. 10:5) with "Go ye into all the world" (Mk. 16:15). Neither of these commissions was given to the Body of Christ. The most obvious reason is that the Body of Christ was not revealed until several years later through Paul.

In this present age God certainly wants the gospel to be preached to every creature and the apostle Paul labored to that end (Col. 1:23). So, how could we possibly say that Mark 16:15 is not our commission?

(15) And he said unto them, Go ye into all the world, and preach the gospel to every creature.
(16) He that believeth and is baptized shall be saved; but he that believeth not shall be damned.
(17) And these signs shall follow them that believe; In my name shall they cast out devils; they shall speak with new tongues;
(18) They shall take up serpents; and if they drink any deadly thing, it shall not hurt them; they shall lay hands on the sick, and they shall recover. (Mk. 16:15-18)

Of all the people who claim that this is our commission, is it not odd that nobody today is actually fulfilling it? They should call it the great OMMISSION. All of the denominations pick what they like and forget the rest.

- The evangelicals focus on v.15.
- The "church of Christ" focuses on vs.16.
- The Charismatics focus on v.17.
- The snake-handling Pentecostals focus on v.18.

There have been people who have literally died trying to follow verse 18! Many have become discouraged and defeated because they cannot do the signs that the passage says will follow them that believe. The way that the scholars try to get around this passage is to claim that it does not belong in the text. Many modern versions have footnotes that cast doubt on the passage.

Imagine the Gospel of Mark ending at verse 8 with the words "they were afraid." If we rightly divide the word of truth, we can leave the passage as it is, and it will make perfect sense.

(9) Now when *Jesus* was risen early the first *day* of the week, he appeared first to Mary Magdalene, out of whom he had cast seven devils.
(10) *And* she went and told them that had been with him, as they mourned and wept.
(11) And they, when they had heard that he was alive, and had been seen of her, believed not.
(12) After that he appeared in another form unto two of them, as they walked, and went into the country.
(13) And they went and told *it* unto the residue: neither believed they them.
(14) Afterward he appeared unto the eleven as they sat at meat, and upbraided them with their unbelief and hardness of heart, because they believed not them which had seen him after he was risen.

On the day that Christ rose from the dead, the disciples were mourning and weeping, not rejoicing. They did not believe the report that He was risen.

(15) And he said unto them, Go ye into all the world, and preach the gospel to every creature.

Who is "them?" The apostles. Which gospel? The gospel that was being preached in this context is the gospel of the kingdom. It was the good news that the prophesied kingdom that God promised Israel was at hand. Christ will reign from Jerusalem over the entire world. Two days before the cross Christ told His disciples that the gospel of the kingdom would be preached in "all the world" (Matt. 24:14). The gospel that Christ revealed to Paul was preached in all the world in the first century (Col. 1:6, 23) and the end still has not come. Do you think Christ was mistaken?

(16) He that believeth and is baptized shall be saved; but he that believeth not shall be damned.

The gospel of the kingdom required the water baptism of repentance for the remission of sins (Mk. 1:4-5). That is the gospel Christ sent the Jewish apostles to preach, which is proven by Peter's message on the Day of Pentecost (Acts 2:38). The water baptism in and of itself did not save them, but it was required as an expression of repentance and faith. Did Christ send the twelve apostles to baptize? Then Paul was not sent under the same commission (1 Cor. 1:17).

(17) And these signs shall follow them that believe; In my name shall they cast out devils; they shall speak with new tongues;
(18) They shall take up serpents; and if they drink any deadly thing, it shall not hurt them; they shall lay hands on the sick, and they shall recover.
(19) So then after the Lord had spoken unto them, he was received up into heaven, and sat on the right hand of God.
(20) And they went forth, and preached every where, the Lord working with *them*, and confirming the word with signs following. Amen.

Christ did not say, "These signs MIGHT follow them that believe." The Bible teaches that the Jews require a sign (1 Cor.

1:22; Ps. 74:9; Jn. 4:48). The nation of Israel began with the signs of healing and snake handling (Ex. 4:1-9). The gospel of the kingdom is accompanied with signs of the kingdom (Heb. 2:3-5).

1) Cast out devils – Rev. 20:1-3
2) Speak with new tongues – Zeph. 3:9; Zech. 8:22-23
3) Take up deadly serpents – Isa. 11:8-9; Lk. 10:19; Rev. 9:19
4) Drink deadly thing – Rev. 8:8-11; 16:4
5) Lay hands on the sick – Isa. 32:24

The kingdom has been postponed and the signs have ceased (1 Cor. 13:8-13). Paul worked signs during the Acts period to prove his apostleship (2 Cor. 12:12). The twelve apostles did not fulfill their commission in the first century, but it will be fulfilled by the 144,000 in the future tribulation period (Rev. 7).

There are other passages concerning the kingdom commission. Christ made appearances to His disciples over a forty-day period between His resurrection and public ascension. He commissioned them at different times and in different places. All of them concern the kingdom, but there are distinctions. There are things about each passage that do not apply today.

- Matt. 28:18-20 – Teach the law (Isa. 2:1-5; Matt. 5:17-20)
- Lk. 24:46-49 – Power from on high to do signs (Isa. 32:15)
- Jn. 20:21-23 – Authority to remit and retain sins (Matt. 18:18)
- Acts 1:6-8 – Begin in Jerusalem (Jer. 3:17)

So then, what is our commission? It is clearly stated in the following passage.

(14) For the love of Christ constraineth us; because we thus judge, that if one died for all, then were all dead:
(15) And *that* he died for all, that they which live should not henceforth live unto themselves, but unto him which died for them, and rose again.
(16) Wherefore henceforth know we no man after the flesh: yea, though we have known Christ after the flesh, yet now henceforth know we *him* no more.
(17) Therefore if any man *be* in Christ, *he is* a new creature: old things are passed away; behold, all things are become new.
(18) And all things *are* of God, who hath reconciled us to himself by Jesus Christ, and hath given to us the ministry of reconciliation;
(19) To wit, that God was in Christ, reconciling the world unto himself, not imputing their trespasses unto them; and <u>hath committed unto us the word of reconciliation.</u>
(20) Now then we are ambassadors for Christ, as though God did beseech *you* by us: we pray *you* in Christ's stead, be ye reconciled to God.
(21) For he hath made him *to be* sin for us, who knew no sin; that we might be made the righteousness of God in him. (2 Cor. 5:14-21)

There are Different Baptisms in the Bible

The failure to rightly divide the different commissions in the Bible is the reason that most denominations require water baptism for either salvation or church membership.

Water baptism has long been a controversial subject that the professing church has been divided over. There is no majority agreement in the professing church concerning how to answer basic questions about water baptism. Is it to be done by immersion, sprinkling, or pouring? Is it for salvation, church membership, or testimony? Who has the authority to baptize? What words are to be said during the baptismal ceremony? Another legitimate but rarely asked question is, does water baptism matter today?

Why all the confusion? Most do not rightly divide the word of truth and consider what Paul says (2 Tim. 2:7, 15). If water baptism were an ordinance in this present age of grace, don't you think Paul would have said so and given us instruction concerning it?

What is baptism? Many will say it means immersion in water. That may be how some dictionaries define it, but that is not how the King James Bible defines it. The nation of Israel was baptized unto Moses when they crossed the Red Sea, and they did not get wet at all (1 Cor 10:1-2). This baptism teaches us that baptism is an identification and not immersion in water. After all, how could a baptism with fire be immersion in water?

Let's consider the first passage in which baptism is mentioned.

(1) In those days came John the Baptist, preaching in the wilderness of Judaea,
(2) And saying, Repent ye: for the kingdom of heaven is at hand.
(3) For this is he that was spoken of by the prophet Esaias, saying, The voice of one crying in the wilderness, Prepare ye the way of the Lord, make his paths straight.

Study Notes

(4) And the same John had his raiment of camel's hair, and a leathern girdle about his loins; and his meat was locusts and wild honey.
(5) Then went out to him Jerusalem, and all Judaea, and all the region round about Jordan,
(6) And were baptized of him in Jordan, confessing their sins.
(7) But when he saw many of the Pharisees and Sadducees come to his baptism, he said unto them, O generation of vipers, who hath warned you to flee from the wrath to come?
(8) Bring forth therefore fruits meet for repentance:
(9) And think not to say within yourselves, We have Abraham to *our* father: for I say unto you, that God is able of these stones to raise up children unto Abraham.
(10) And now also the axe is laid unto the root of the trees: therefore every tree which bringeth not forth good fruit is hewn down, and cast into the fire. (Matt. 3:1-10)

John, the forerunner of the King, baptized repentant Jews for the remission of sins. Baptism was required to prove repentance and faith under the gospel of the kingdom (Mk. 1:4-5; Mk. 16:16; Acts 2:38). This baptism was to manifest Christ to Israel (Jn. 1:31) and was a ceremonial washing and purification (Jn. 3:23-26).

(11) I indeed baptize you with water unto repentance: but he that cometh after me is mightier than I, whose shoes I am not worthy to bear: he shall baptize you with the Holy Ghost, and *with* fire:
(12) Whose fan *is* in his hand, and he will throughly purge his floor, and gather his wheat into the garner; but he will burn up the chaff with unquenchable fire. (Matt. 3:11-12)

There are three baptisms mentioned in one verse:
1) With water - for purification
2) With the Holy Ghost - for power
3) With fire - for punishment

(13) Then cometh Jesus from Galilee to Jordan unto John, to be baptized of him.
(14) But John forbad him, saying, I have need to be baptized of thee, and comest thou to me?
(15) And Jesus answering said unto him, Suffer *it to be so* **now: for thus it becometh us to fulfil all righteousness. Then he suffered him.**
(16) And Jesus, when he was baptized, went up straightway out of the water: and, lo, the heavens were opened unto him, and he saw the Spirit of God descending like a dove, and lighting upon him:
(17) And lo a voice from heaven, saying, This is my beloved Son, in whom I am well pleased. (Matt. 3:13-17)

We cannot follow Christ in baptism, because His was unique. He was identifying with the sinners He came to save. This is the beginning of His ministry. According to the law, priests were to be washed and anointed when they entered their priestly office (Ex. 29:1-4, 7). Christ came to fulfill the law (Matt. 5:17; Heb. 9:10).

Christ spoke of a baptism He had to be baptized with AFTER He was baptized with water (Lk. 12:50). He was referring to His suffering on the cross. He also told the disciples that they would be baptized with suffering (Matt. 20:20-23).

The mystery of the church which is the Body of Christ was revealed to the apostle Paul. The spiritual baptism that makes us members of one Body is only found in his epistles (1 Cor. 12:13).

We have seen seven different baptisms in the word of God:
1) Baptism unto Moses
2) Baptism unto repentance
3) Baptism of Christ
4) Baptism with the Holy Ghost
5) Baptism with fire
6) Baptism of suffering
7) Baptism into the Body of Christ

(1) I therefore, the prisoner of the Lord, beseech you that ye walk worthy of the vocation wherewith ye are called,
(2) With all lowliness and meekness, with longsuffering, forbearing one another in love;
(3) Endeavouring to keep the unity of the Spirit in the bond of peace.
(4) *There is* one body, and one Spirit, even as ye are called in one hope of your calling;
(5) One Lord, one faith, one baptism,
(6) One God and Father of all, who *is* above all, and through all, and in you all. (Eph. 4:1-6)

Which baptism was Paul referring to when he said there is "one baptism?" It cannot be water baptism because water cannot put you in Christ. The seven things mentioned in the passage are all spiritual. There is only one baptism by which one Spirit baptizes believers into one Body. Paul mentioned water baptism one time in his epistles, and in that passage, he certainly did not teach that it was an ordinance for today.

(10) Now I beseech you, brethren, by the name of our Lord Jesus Christ, that ye all speak the same thing, and *that* there be no divisions among you; but *that* ye be perfectly joined together in the same mind and in the same judgment.
(11) For it hath been declared unto me of you, my brethren, by them *which are of the house* of Chloe, that there are contentions among you.
(12) Now this I say, that every one of you saith, I am of Paul; and I of Apollos; and I of Cephas; and I of Christ.
(13) Is Christ divided? was Paul crucified for you? or were ye baptized in the name of Paul?
(14) I thank God that I baptized none of you, but Crispus and Gaius;
(15) Lest any should say that I had baptized in mine own name.
(16) And I baptized also the household of Stephanas: besides, I know not whether I baptized any other.
(17) For Christ sent me not to baptize, but to preach the gospel: not with wisdom of words, lest the cross of Christ should be made of none effect. (1 Cor. 1:10-17)

Yes, Paul baptized a few people in the transition period recorded in the book of Acts, but he never commanded it. There is no explanation given as to why he did it. The book of Acts is a history book that records the fall and diminishing of Israel. We must look to Paul's epistles for our doctrine and practice as a church. That Paul was sent not to baptize proves he was given a distinct message and ministry from that of John the Baptist and the twelve apostles who were sent to baptize (Jn. 1:33; Matt. 28:19).

There is only one baptism that matters today, and it is the spiritual one that God performs the moment we trust Christ as our Saviour (Rom. 6:3-4; 1 Cor. 12:13; Gal. 3:27-28; Col. 2:10-12).

There are Different Raptures in the Bible

The English word *rapture* refers to a state or experience of being carried away. It is from the Latin *rapto* which means to seize or snatch away something by force. It is not a Bible word, but it is a good term to use in referring to the biblical doctrine of being caught up to heaven. Those who are alive when Christ comes will not have to die; we will be "caught up" and changed.

(50) Now this I say, brethren, that flesh and blood cannot inherit the kingdom of God; neither doth corruption inherit incorruption.
(51) Behold, I shew you a mystery; We shall not all sleep, but we shall all be changed,
(52) In a moment, in the twinkling of an eye, at the last trump: for the trumpet shall sound, and the dead shall be raised incorruptible, and we shall be changed.
(1 Cor. 15:50-52)

(13) But I would not have you to be ignorant, brethren, concerning them which are asleep, that ye sorrow not, even as others which have no hope.
(14) For if we believe that Jesus died and rose again, even so them also which sleep in Jesus will God bring with him.
(15) For this we say unto you by the word of the Lord, that we which are alive *and* remain unto the coming of the Lord shall not prevent them which are asleep.

(16) For the Lord himself shall descend from heaven with a shout, with the voice of the archangel, and with the trump of God: and the dead in Christ shall rise first:
(17) Then we which are alive *and* remain shall be caught up together with them in the clouds, to meet the Lord in the air: and so shall we ever be with the Lord.
(18) Wherefore comfort one another with these words.
(1 Thess. 4:13-18)

This present age began with a sudden glorious appearing when the message of grace came down and Saul of Tarsus was saved on the road to Damascus (Acts 9:1-9; Titus 2:11), and it will end with a sudden glorious appearing of Christ when the Body of Christ, made up of all those who believed the gospel of the grace of God, is caught up to meet the Lord in the air (Titus 2:13).

In the Bible, hope is a certain expectation of what God has promised. Israel's hope is for the Lord to resurrect them and give them a kingdom on the earth (Joel 3:16; Rev. 20:4-6). Sadly, most professing Christians do not know what the hope of their calling is because they think they are Israel (Eph. 1:15-18; 4:4).

We are to be looking for Christ to come at any moment and take us up to be with Him in glory (Phil. 3:20-21; Col. 1:27; 3:1-4). We will reign with Christ in heavenly places (Eph. 2:6-7; 2 Cor. 5:1).

There are other raptures in the Bible. Failure to rightly divide the different raptures will rob you of your blessed hope.

Three raptures yet to come:
1) Before the tribulation period – Body of Christ (2 Thess. 2:13-14)

2) During the tribulation period – 144,000 (Rev. 12:5; 14:1-5)
3) After the tribulation period – Israel to their land (Matt. 24:29-31)

The Body of Christ is a mystery that was hid from the prophets, therefore we will not be here during the prophesied seventieth week of Daniel which is about Israel and the nations (Dan. 9:24-27). Paul never taught us to look for the signs of the second coming of Christ. When he outlined the tribulation period in 2 Thessalonians 2, it was to show that we will not be here for those events.

False teachers were troubling the church at Thessalonica by saying they were in the day of the Lord. Paul wrote to correct that false doctrine and comfort the saints with sound doctrine (2 Thess. 2:13-17). When Paul told the Thessalonians that the Lord would keep them from evil (2 Thess. 3:3), he was writing to believers who were being greatly persecuted. Therefore, he must have been referring to the evil of the antichrist. We are not appointed to wrath and therefore we will be saved from the wrath to come in the future tribulation period through the rapture.

(8) But let us, who are of the day, be sober, putting on the breastplate of faith and love; and for an helmet, the hope of salvation.
(9) For God hath not appointed us to wrath, but to obtain salvation by our Lord Jesus Christ,
(10) Who died for us, that, whether we wake or sleep, we should live together with him.
(11) Wherefore comfort yourselves together, and edify one another, even as also ye do. (1 Thess. 5:8-11)

We are to be waiting and looking for Christ from heaven, and not the antichrist from the earth (1 Cor. 1:7; Phil. 3:20-21; 1 Thess. 1:10; 2 Thess. 3:5; Titus 2:13). The key to understanding our blessed hope is recognizing Paul's distinct ministry. There are major differences between this present dispensation and the future tribulation period, not the least of which is the different gospels that are preached (cf. Matt. 24:14; Gal. 1:6-12).

Those who try to teach the pre-tribulation rapture from passages outside of Paul's epistles are hindering the truth. For example, Jesus Christ was not talking about our rapture in Matthew 24:36-42. The ones taken are taken away in judgment (Lk. 17:34-37), and the ones who remain will go into the kingdom. There are some today that have been swayed away from our blessed hope because of this type of inconsistent dispensationalism.

We must not confound the rapture of the Body of Christ with the revelation of Jesus Christ (Rev. 1:1, 7).

The Rapture	The Revelation
Mystery revealed to Paul	Spoken by the prophets
Before the tribulation	After the tribulation
Christ comes secretly to meet us in the air	Christ comes publicly to earth
No signs precede	Signs precede
Christ comes in blessing	Christ comes in judgment
For His Body	For Israel
Judgment Seat of Christ	Judgment on Nations
Rapture to heaven	Rapture to the Land

There are Many Other Differences in the Bible

Here is a list of twenty-three examples that prove you cannot follow everything the Bible says, and that it must be rightly divided to be understood.

Compare:
1) The Gospel – Matt. 4:23; 17:22-23; 24:14 with Acts 20:24; 1 Cor. 15:3-4; Col. 1:5-6
2) The Audience – Matt. 10:5-7; Lk. 24:47; Acts 11:19 with Acts 26:17; 1 Tim. 2:4
3) Salvation - Mk. 16:16; Acts 2:38 with Acts 16:30-31; Eph. 2:8-9
4) Justification - Jam. 2:24 with Rom. 3:28; 4:5
5) Righteousness - Deut. 6:24-25; Lk. 1:6; Rev. 19:8 with Phil. 3:4-10
6) Forgiveness - Matt. 6:14-15 with Eph. 4:32
7) Acceptance - Acts 10:35 with Titus 3:5; Eph. 1:6
8) Love of God - Jn. 15:10; Jude 21 with Rom. 8:38-39
9) Security - Matt. 24:13 with 1 Cor. 1:8
10) Sealed with Spirit - 1 Sam. 16:14; Ps. 51:11 with Eph. 4:30
11) Blessings - Deut. 28:1-5 with Eph. 1:3
12) Coming of the Lord - Matt.24:15 (signs) with Phil. 3:20 (no signs)
13) Law - Matt. 23:1-3 with Rom. 6:14
14) Diet - Lev. 11:46-47 with 1 Tim. 4:1-6
15) Circumcision - Gen. 17:9-14 with Gal. 5:2
16) Holy days - Lev. 23:1-3 with Gal. 4:8-11; Col. 2:16
17) Water Baptism - Matt. 28:19 with 1 Cor. 1:17
18) Signs - Mk. 16:17-18 with 1 Cor. 13:8-13
19) Teachers - 1 Jn. 2:27 with Eph. 4:11
20) Prayer - Matt. 21:22 with 2 Cor. 12:8-9

21) Provision - Acts 4:34-35 with 1 Thess. 4:11-12
22) Riches - Matt. 19:21-24; Jam. 5:1 with 1 Tim. 6:17-19
23) Giving - Mal. 3:6-10 with 2 Cor. 9:7

Chapter 15
Dispensational Salvation

One of the most important things about rightly dividing the word of truth is that it enables us to understand and clearly present the only gospel by which sinners are saved in this present age. Yet, one of the biggest problems that people have with dispensationalism concerns the issue of salvation in different ages because the common and traditional view is that salvation is the same for all people in all ages.

Most professing Christians believe there is only one gospel in the Bible, not because they personally studied the matter, but because that is what they have always heard.

The common belief is that people in the Old Testament were saved by looking toward the cross and people in the New Testament are saved by looking back to the cross. How can that be true when the twelve apostles were not looking toward the cross? The fact that they had been preaching the gospel (Lk. 9:1-6) for three years before Christ began to speak to them about His death, burial, and resurrection, and that they did not understand or believe it (Lk. 18:31-34), proves that there are different gospels in the Bible.

There is much confusion on this issue, and some of the blame is to be laid at the feet of dispensational teachers who make it sound like salvation is by works in other dispensations. God has never and will never accept the works of sinful flesh as a basis for salvation.

It is the spirit that quickeneth; the flesh profiteth nothing: the words that I speak unto you, *they* are spirit, and *they* are life. (Jn. 6:63)

For I know that in me (that is, in my flesh,) dwelleth no good thing: for to will is present with me; but *how* to perform that which is good I find not. (Rom. 7:18)

So then they that are in the flesh cannot please God. (Rom. 8:8)

Please carefully consider the following five points that will help you to better understand the dispensational truth of the word of God concerning salvation.

1) The basis of salvation in every age is the blood of Christ.

The death and resurrection of Christ is the only basis upon which God can save a sinner in any age. It was planned before the world began and prophesied in the Old Testament. However, it was not understood or preached as good news until after it was accomplished. Its full meaning was a mystery revealed through Paul's gospel (Gal. 1:11-12). The cross-work of Christ is the secret to God's dealings with sinners in every age, but it was not fully revealed until this present age.

By faith, the OT saints obeyed the commandments of the law and brought the required sacrifices for their sins. Through forbearance, God allowed the blood of bulls and goats to cover sins (Heb. 10:4) because He knew the blood of Christ would be shed for the remission of sins (Rom. 3:25).

2) The condition for salvation in every age is essentially faith.

Without faith, it is impossible to please God (Heb. 11:6). The eleventh chapter of Hebrews demonstrates that people before the law and under the law obtained a good report from God by faith.

3) The object of faith in every age is the word of God.

Faith is not merely believing something. Everybody believes in something, but not everybody has faith (2 Thess. 3:2). Faith is believing the word of God (Rom. 4:3-5; 10:17).

4) The content of faith is not the same in every age because God has not given man the same message in every age.

We have already seen that there are different gospel messages for different ages. God has not always told men not to do any works but to only trust the finished work of Christ alone for salvation as He does in this age (Rom. 3:28; 4:5).

In time past, He required works of men to prove their faith, and He will do so again after this age. If God requires works, real faith will seek to do those works, but the works in and of themselves have never and will never save a sinner. A man's faith must be proven. That explains what James taught the "twelve tribes" (Jam. 1:1) concerning being justified by faith and works (Jam. 2:14-26).

Why doesn't God require us to do works to prove our faith in this age? We are justified "by the faith of Christ" (Gal. 2:16) and His faith was perfect and proven. Yes, we must believe on the Lord Jesus Christ to receive salvation (Acts 16:31), but we are justified based on what Christ accomplished for us through being obedient unto death, even the death of the cross (Phil. 2:8).

5) The results of faith are not the same in every age because God has not given believers in every age the same position, blessings, and destiny.

There is doctrine revealed in Paul's epistles concerning the position, blessings, and destiny of the Body of Christ that we do not find in the Old Testament, Gospels, or Hebrews through Revelation. This information is only found in Paul's epistles because he is the one to whom the glorified Christ from Heaven revealed it. Christ committed these truths to Paul to make them known.

Our position as members of the Body of Christ means that nothing can separate us from the love of God (cf. Rom. 8:35-39 with John 15:10 and Jude 21). We are sealed with the Holy Spirit (Eph. 1:13) and therefore would never have to pray, "take not thy holy spirit from me" as David did (Ps. 51:11). The Spirit of the Lord will never depart from us as He did from King Saul (cf. 1 Sam. 16:14 with Eph. 4:30). We are never told to endure unto the end (Matt. 24:13), but rather that Christ will confirm us unto the end (1 Cor. 1:8). Our blessings are spiritual and in heavenly places (Eph. 1:3), not material blessings on earth (Deut. 28:1-14).

We did not obtain our blessings by keeping the commandments of the law but by virtue of our standing in Christ. The Body of Christ is destined to reign with Christ in heavenly places (Eph. 2:6-7; 2 Tim. 4:18). It is Israel that is destined to reign on the earth (Ex. 19:5-6; Rev. 5:10).

The Faith of Christ

One of the great and distinctive truths that the Lord revealed through the apostle Paul for this present age of grace is what has been accomplished for the Body of Christ by the faith of Christ.

Paul referred to the faith of Christ seven times in his thirteen epistles. Yet, this great truth has been removed in the modern versions of the Bible. They all change the faith of Christ to faith in Christ. Just changing a little two-letter word can make a BIG difference in Bible doctrine!

We cannot be saved without putting our faith in Christ (e.g., Gal. 3:26), but there is a difference between faith IN Christ and the faith OF Christ. It should not be surprising that the new versions omit this great truth since they attack the person and work of Christ in a number of passages.

There are different kinds of faith in the Bible (the context determines the meaning).
1. The faith God has revealed to man – a body of doctrine (Rom. 1:5)
2. The faith of God – God's faithfulness and trustworthiness (Rom. 3:3-4)
3. The faith of a man in God – believing the word of God (Rom. 1:8; 4:3-5; 10:17)

The faith of Christ covers all three, but the apostle Paul is the only writer who speaks of sinners being instantly and permanently justified by the faith of Christ. The epistle of James and the book of Revelation refer to the faith of Jesus Christ, but both references refer to the doctrine Christ taught in His earthly ministry (Jam. 2:1; Rev. 14:12).

Since Jesus Christ is God, why did He need faith? When Christ was born into this world, He was fully God, and yet He was fully man. As a man, He believed His Father and was perfectly obedient to carry out His will (Titus 1:1-3; Phil. 2:5-8; Heb. 10:5-7). In the Gospel of John, a book that emphasizes the deity of Christ, we find the Lord continually referring to His dependence and obedience to the Father (e.g., Jn. 5:17-20, 30; 8:28-29). By faith, Christ prayed in the garden, "not my will, but thine, be done" in regard to taking the cup which represented God pouring out His wrath on the sin of the world. He knew that He would be raised from the dead and that through His death, burial, and resurrection He would accomplish salvation for all who would believe on Him.

Please carefully read the following references in their surrounding context.

- **Rom. 3:21-22** – The righteousness of God by faith of Jesus Christ was witnessed in the OT, not revealed and explained, BUT NOW is made manifest through the preaching committed to Paul.
- **Gal. 2:16** – God cannot declare a man righteous based on his flesh doing the works of the law (for all have sinned), but He does so by the faith of Jesus Christ which accomplished justification for us by grace.

- **Gal. 2:20** – We are not only justified by the faith of Christ, but we also live by the faith of the Son of God. The Christian life is Christ living His life through us.
- **Gal. 3:22-24** – There was faith in the OT (see Heb. 11), but justification by the faith of Christ was revealed through Paul's ministry.
- **Eph. 3:12** – Because of the faith of Christ, we have the same full and free access to the Father as His beloved Son (Gal. 4:6; Eph. 1:6).
- **Phil. 3:9** – The righteousness that we try to produce in the flesh is but dung (vv.4-8) compared to the righteousness available to us by the faith of Christ.

The difference between Paul and James on the issue of justification (cf. Rom. 3:28 with Jam. 2:24) is that Paul talks about justification by the faith of Christ, which is perfect and proven, and therefore our justification is instant and permanent; while James talks about justification by the faith of a man, which must be tested and proven by works, and is therefore a process. Paul and James are writing to different groups (cf. Rom. 11:13 with Jam. 1:1) in different dispensations about different gospels.

How many churches believe and teach about what has been accomplished for us by the faith of Christ? Sadly, not many because most do not rightly divide the word of truth and recognize the new revelations that Christ gave the apostle Paul for this present age.

Being grounded in this great doctrine produces much assurance of salvation and eternal security (Col. 2:10). Our faith is often weak and wavering, but the faith of Christ is perfect and already proven. Rest in what He accomplished for you by His faith.

Chapter 16
What About Signs?

There is much confusion and controversy in the professing church concerning the issue of signs due to a failure to rightly divide the word of truth. The following twelve points provide a basic overview concerning the dispensational purpose of signs in the Bible.

1) Signs are supernatural manifestations associated with miracles and wonders (Acts 2:22; Heb. 2:1-5) that are given to confirm what God has said (Mk. 16:20).

2) Satan can counterfeit signs (2 Thess. 2:9; Deut. 13:1-5), therefore the word of God is far more important than signs (2 Pet. 1:16-21).

3) The nation of Israel, God's earthly people, began with signs (Ex. 4:1-9, 29-31) and God uses signs in His dealings with them (Ps. 74:9; Jn. 4:48; 1 Cor. 1:22).

4) Christ worked signs in fulfillment of prophecy and in accordance with His message (Matt. 11:1-6), not merely to prove He was the Son of God.

5) The signs pointed to the promised kingdom that was at hand. The gospel of the kingdom is accompanied by signs of the kingdom (Matt. 4:17, 23-24; Lk. 8:1).

6) Signs continued in the Acts period even after Israel fell because God used Paul's ministry to get a remnant out of Israel and into the Body of Christ (Rom. 11:1-5, 11-15) as they were being diminished throughout the transition period. Paul had the signs of an apostle (2 Cor. 12:12), but he did not preach the gospel of the kingdom.

7) God gave Gentile believers sign gifts during the Acts period to provoke the Jews (1 Cor. 12:1-11). The church at Corinth was started next door to a synagogue (Acts 18:1-8).

8) The carnal Corinthians misused the sign gifts (1 Cor. 12-14). For example, they exalted the gift of tongues above the gift of prophecy. Tongues, the supernatural ability to speak in other languages, was a sign to the unbelieving Jews (1 Cor. 14:21-22). Nobody today who imagines they have the gift of tongues follows the rules for tongues speaking (1 Cor. 14:27-40), which proves they are not led of the Spirit.

9) During the Acts period, Paul said that the sign gifts would cease (1 Cor. 13:8-13).

10) The signs ceased when Israel was officially set aside in judicial blindness (Acts 28:25-28) and the apostle Paul fulfilled the word of God ("that which is perfect," 1 Cor. 13:10; Col. 1:25). Paul no longer had the gift of healing after the Acts period (2 Tim. 4:20).

11) The complete word of God is all-sufficient for the ministry (1 Cor. 14:3; 2 Tim. 3:16-17). To desire signs over the

scripture is childish (1 Cor. 14:20). To look for signs in this present age will lead to deception. The Body of Christ, God's heavenly people, is to "walk by faith, not by sight" (2 Cor. 5:7).

12) God will use signs in the tribulation period when He resumes His dealings with Israel (e.g., Rev. 11:1-6). The kingdom commission that Christ gave His Jewish apostles was postponed with the revelation of the mystery but will yet be fulfilled (Matt. 24:14; Mk. 16:15-18).

Chapter 17
A Word of Caution

Once we are on the right track of rightly dividing the word of truth, we must be careful to avoid some pitfalls that we will encounter along the way.

The Failure to see the Connections in the Bible

Some believe and teach that dispensations are cut-and-dried time-periods that are disconnected and isolated from one another. They focus on the divisions in the Bible to the point that they neglect, if not ignore or deny, the connections in the Bible. Because most preachers only focus on connections in the Bible, some overcorrect in their effort to avoid that extreme and go to the other extreme of only focusing on the divisions. They have imagined an unbiblical and unbalanced either/or ultimatum in Bible study: there are either divisions or connections, but there cannot be both.

What will happen to those young in the faith who are taught this faulty concept when false teachers come along and point out legitimate connections in the Bible? They may begin to think dispensationalism is wrong and start listening to the false teacher.

C.R. Stam warned many years ago, *"Much harm and loss has come to the church because God's "workmen" have failed to note distinctions and divisions in the Word of Truth. But serious harm can and does also result from a failure to recognize the unity of God's great plan for the ages; from a failure to observe connections as well as divisions. Extreme dispensationalists see many distinctions in the scriptures – even distinctions that do not exist! – but they fail to see some of the most important connections."* (Things that Differ, pg. 249)

Is it possible for there to be both connections and distinctions concerning the same thing? Yes, and here are some examples:
1) There is one God who exists in three persons (1 Jn. 5:7).
2) The Bible is 66 books in one book.
3) In the Body of Christ, there are many different members in one Body (1 Cor. 12:12-13).
4) Throughout eternity there will be one family of God in heaven and earth (Eph. 1:10; 3:14-15).

Extreme dispensationalists go beyond the apostle Paul in how they divide the word of God. It is this kind of extremism that causes them to assert things like:

- *Nobody today is born again* – While Christ and Peter were referring to Israel when they used the term "born again" (Jn. 3:3, 7; 1 Pet. 1:23), the apostle Paul taught that believers in this age are "born after the Spirit" (Gal. 4:29) and regenerated by the Holy Ghost (Titus 3:5). The differences in doctrine between Israel and the Body of Christ concerning this matter does not negate the spiritual application that can be made of the term to us today. All who are born into the world are born of the flesh. When we get saved, we are regenerated by the Spirit. Therefore, we may apply the term "born again."

Study Notes

- *We are not saved by the blood of the New Testament* – While the Body of Christ is not under the new covenant, which will be made with Israel at the second coming of Christ (Heb. 8:8-13), we are saved by the blood of the New Testament (1 Cor. 11:23-26; 2 Cor. 3:6). There is a difference between a covenant and a testament. For example, death is required for a testament (Heb. 9:16-17), but not for a covenant.

- *The Lord's Supper is not for today* – The apostle Paul received the Lord's Supper by divine revelation and delivered it to the church to be kept as a memorial of the death of Christ (1 Cor. 11:17-34). If the Lord's Supper were the same thing as the Last Supper, why would Paul need to receive it by divine revelation? If the Lord's Supper is not for today, why would Paul bother to write a lengthy passage to correct the misuse of it? The Lord's Supper is a simple memorial that pictures the physical body of Christ that was crucified for us and partaking of it together as a church symbolizes the communion of the spiritual Body of Christ that is formed based on the cross (1 Cor. 10:16-17).

- *We are not in the book of life* – All who have eternal life are written in the book of life, including those in the Body of Christ (Phil. 4:3). The difference is that Paul never gives us any warning of being blotted out of it because we are sealed with the Spirit (Eph. 4:30) unlike what we find in the book of Revelation concerning the tribulation period (Rev. 3:5).

The revelation of a new dispensation does not automatically negate everything from previous dispensations. When God changes something, He says so. In other words, some things carry over from one dispensation to another which is why Paul said that ALL scripture is profitable for us today (2 Tim. 3:16). While there are things that do not mix, such as law and grace, there are doctrines and moral principles that do not change through the ages. We could not understand much in Paul's Epistles without the rest of scripture because he referred to other scripture many times.

How do we know the difference between what is connected and what must be divided? We are to consider what Paul said first since God spoke through him directly to us in this present age, and then we must rightly divide the things in the Bible that differ from what Paul wrote to us (2 Tim. 2:7, 15). The simple rule is what God has divided, leave divided and what God has connected, leave connected.

Please read and carefully consider the following references which provide examples of how Paul made connections between this present dispensation and other dispensations.

1) Innocence – Rom. 5:12-19; 2 Cor. 11:3; Eph. 5:31; 1 Tim. 2:12-14
2) Conscience – Rom. 2:14-15 (Paul used the word "conscience" 20 times)
3) Human Government – Rom. 13:1-7 (still in effect today)
4) Promise – Rom. 4; Gal. 3 (spiritual application)
5) Law – Rom. 3:19-20; 7:7-14; 13:8-10; Gal. 3:23-25; 1 Tim. 1:8

6) Kingdom – Rom. 15:1-13 (spiritual application of kingdom prophecies)
7) Fulness of times – Eph. 1:10 (when God's purposes for the times will all be brought to perfect fruition, all gathered together in Christ)

The Lord Jesus Christ is central in all the scriptures (Lk. 24:27, 44; Jn. 5:39, 46; 16:12-15). He is the foundation of both the prophetic kingdom program of Israel (1 Pet. 2:6) and the mystery program of the Body of Christ (1 Cor. 3:10-11). Christ connects all of the dispensations because He revealed them, and they concern Him (Rom. 11:33-36).

Beware of Hyper-Dispensationalism

The term "hyper-dispensationalism" is an intimidating word, but it is not difficult to understand. The Greek prefix "hyper" means excessive and going beyond what is right and acceptable. Some prefer the Latin prefix "ultra." Man is always prone to extremes, so it is certainly possible to go to unscriptural extremes and be guilty of *wrongly dividing* the word of truth.

Doctrinally speaking, the issue of when you believe this present dispensation began is typically one of the main ways people judge whether or not they think someone is a hyper-dispensationalist. This is understandable because what we believe about this issue has major doctrinal and practical ramifications.

If you believe that this present dispensation began with Paul's salvation and ministry, other dispensationalists who hold to the traditional view that it started on the Day of Pentecost (Acts 2) will accuse you of being a hyper-dispensationalist. They typically lump our view together with those who believe the Body of Christ started in Acts 28:28, which actually is hyper-dispensationalism.

Be it known therefore unto you, that the salvation of God is sent unto the Gentiles, and that they will hear it. (Acts 28:28)

The Acts 28 position is the result of misunderstanding Paul's ministry in the Acts period. We must keep in mind that Acts is a historical record of the transition period in which God moved from the nation of Israel to the Body of Christ; from the gospel of the kingdom (Acts 2:38) to the gospel of the grace of God (Acts 13:38-39); from the ministry of Peter (Acts 1-12) to that of Paul (Acts 13-28). God used Paul's ministry to call out a remnant of Israel by grace (Rom. 11:1-6) before He set the nation aside in blindness. That is why Paul went "to the Jew first" (Rom. 1:16) throughout his Acts ministry. The Body of Christ began historically in the Acts period but there are some differences between Paul's ministry during the transition and afterward. For example, it is evident that he no longer had the spiritual gift of healing after the Acts period (Phil. 2:25-27; 2 Tim. 4:20).

The Acts 28ers see the differences between Paul's ministry in Acts and afterward and then jump to the faulty conclusion that the Body of Christ had not yet been revealed. This is legitimate hyper-dispensationalism because it is going beyond God's scriptural divisions and inventing your own, and it leads to some serious doctrinal problems. It is possible to WRONGLY DIVIDE the word of truth.

We will not take the time here to thoroughly examine and expose the Acts 28 position. It is easy to refute the claim that Paul received the revelation of the Body of Christ after Acts 28:28 by simply reading what he said about the Body of Christ in his epistles that were written BEFORE Acts 28:28.

The following verses were all written before Acts 28.

So we, being many, are one body in Christ, and every one members one of another. (Rom. 12:5)

(12) For as the body is one, and hath many members, and all the members of that one body, being many, are one body: so also is Christ.
(13) For by one Spirit are we all baptized into one body, whether we be Jews or Gentiles, whether we be bond or free; and have been all made to drink into one Spirit.
(1 Cor. 12:12-13)

(27) For as many of you as have been baptized into Christ have put on Christ.
(28) There is neither Jew nor Greek, there is neither bond nor free, there is neither male nor female: for ye are all one in Christ Jesus. (Gal. 3:27-28)

There are also those who may not be Acts 28ers but go to the extreme of believing that only Paul's epistles contain doctrine for this age. They seem to forget that Paul himself said that "All scripture is given by inspiration of God, and is profitable for doctrine" (2 Tim. 3:16). To overemphasize Paul's epistles to the neglect of the rest of scripture is extremism.

There are divisions in the Bible, but it is still ONE BOOK that reveals one true and living God, one set of moral principles, and one great plan of redemption by the blood of Christ.

Practical Hyper-Dispensationalism

It is possible to not be *hyper* in our doctrine but *hyper* in how we act concerning our doctrine. The apostle Paul said that Christians are to be known for their moderation (Phil. 4:5). What is moderation? It is the avoidance of excess or extremes. It is a good testimony to live a balanced Christian life. This is not easy because the flesh is ever prone to excess and extremes. Finding and maintaining the right balance in the Christian life is difficult. Thankfully, "the Lord is at hand." Some say this means that the coming of the Lord for us is imminent (cf. Phil. 3:20), while others say it means Christ is always near. Both are true. He lives in us, and we can live a balanced Christian life through His strength. He is coming soon to glorify us into His image. We will never struggle again in that glorious day.

Extremism is not only the danger of being excessive in a bad thing, for there is also the subtle danger of taking a good thing too far. Eating is good but eating to an extreme is bad. Consider this bit of practical wisdom from Proverbs: "Hast thou found honey? eat so much as is sufficient for thee, lest thou be filled therewith, and vomit it." (Prov. 25:16). We can apply this proverb to our spiritual diet. The word of God is our spiritual food. David said that the word of God is "sweeter also than honey and the honeycomb" (Ps. 19:10).

Now, please do not misunderstand me, we certainly need to be filled with the word of God (Col. 3:16). But the word of God is not only to be taken in, but it is also to be exercised out in our daily life (1 Tim. 4:6-7). We are to "work out" our own salvation (Phil. 2:12). Knowledge without charity puffs up (1 Cor. 8:1-3). Paul said that without charity we are nothing even if we understand all mysteries and have all knowledge (1 Cor. 13:2). We must not study the Bible just to gain knowledge. We must study the Bible to know God in a real relationship and serve Him according to His will.

We are guilty of practical hyper-dispensationalism when:

1) We neglect the scripture that is not written directly to us.

Those of us who have come to understand that the apostle Paul was given the distinct revelations for this present dispensation need to be careful not to overemphasize his epistles to the point of neglecting the rest of scripture. Recognizing that Paul is the divinely appointed pattern and spokesman for this age is important, and we should emphasize the doctrines revealed through him for today. However, it is possible to take it too far. Romans through Philemon is indeed the word of God, but so is the rest of the Bible.

We should follow Paul's example in this matter. His epistles contain many quotes and allusions to the Old Testament scripture. He said that the things which were written aforetime were written for our learning (Rom. 15:4) and admonition (1 Cor. 10:11). In his last inspired epistle, he said that ALL scripture is profitable (2 Tim. 3:16). All dispensationalists at least give lip service to this fact. Even the most extreme dispensationalists would say we should study the whole Bible, but if they rarely preach spiritual applications or teach doctrine other than dispensational truth, they are acting like a hyper-dispensationalist.

God preserved the whole Bible for a reason (Prov. 30:5; Matt. 4:4). Paul's epistles are not the only place to find doctrine for this age. For example, Paul only implies the virgin birth of Christ because it was already clearly established in the scripture. The same is true with the doctrine of hell. There are spiritual applications for us throughout the whole Bible. Paul said that we are not stablished without "the scriptures of the prophets" (Rom. 16:25-26).

2) We cannot fellowship with those who do not see everything the way we do.

There are some who glory in the truth of the ONE BODY but cannot seem to get along with anybody who does not agree with them on every detail of how they understand dispensational truth. They treat Christians who are not as enlightened as they like they are second-class members of the Body of Christ. Isn't it ironic that there are so many cliques and schisms in the "Grace Movement" (1 Cor. 1:10-13)? Those who lament the error of denominationalism are too often denominational in their attitude and conduct.

We are not to be ecumenical. We should take a strong stand for truth, and there is a time to separate from apostates and heretics; but we should not break fellowship over things like whether or not you believe the twelve apostles are in the Body of Christ. The basis of our fellowship is laid out in Ephesians 4:1-6. Be careful not to develop a critical spirit towards all believers who do not see everything the way you do and nitpick everything you hear. By the way, the mainstream dispensationalists typically will not fellowship with us, so they can also be guilty of practical hyper-dispensationalism.

3) We ignore the practical applications of the doctrine we profess to believe.

Being "under grace" is not just a doctrinal statement: it is a spiritual reality that ought to change the way we live (Rom. 6:14-18; Titus 2:1, 11-15). After laying a doctrinal foundation, the apostle Paul always made practical applications to our daily walk. If you think that preaching biblical separation and exhorting the saints to live godly in this present world is legalism, then you are acting like a hyper-dispensationalist.

The grace message does not free us from the responsibility to live right. It teaches us the right way to go about it. What did it do for Paul?

But by the grace of God, I am what I am: and his grace which *was bestowed* upon me was not in vain, but I labored more abundantly than they all: yet not I, but the grace of God which was with me. (1 Cor. 15:10)

If we are going to avoid the pitfall of becoming a hyper-dispensationalist, we must not only know that we live in the Spirit, but we must also walk in the Spirit.

If we live in the Spirit, let us also walk in the Spirit. (Gal. 5:25)

Chapter 18
Defending Dispensational Truth

The truth of God's word does not need us to defend it for it always has and always will stand on its own.

For we can do nothing against the truth, but for the truth. (2 Cor. 13:8)

However, it is clear from the example and teaching of the apostle Paul that we should defend the truth for the sake of helping others. Rightly dividing the word of truth is the key to understanding the Bible. It is the remedy for all the confusion and schisms that plague the professing church.

- By inspiration of God, Paul wrote much scripture in defense of his distinct apostleship and ministry that he received of the Lord (e.g., 2 Cor. 10-13; Gal. 1-2).
- He was "set for the defense of the gospel" (Phil. 1:17).
- He said concerning the legalists who attacked his message of grace, "To whom we gave place by subjection, no, not for an hour; that the truth of the gospel might continue with you." (Gal. 2:5)
- He taught that the church is to be the "pillar and ground of the truth" (1 Tim. 3:15) and that an elder must hold fast to the faithful word that he "may be able by sound doctrine both to exhort and convince the gainsayers." (Titus 1:9)

- He exhorted the Body of Christ to "Let your speech be always with grace, seasoned with salt, that he may know how he ought to answer every man." (Col. 4:6)
- We are to be good soldiers of Christ (2 Tim. 2:3), fighting the good fight of faith (1 Tim. 6:12). We are to put on the whole armor of God and stand for the truth (Eph. 6:10-20).

Dispensationalism in general has always been attacked by the religious world because the mainline denominations think the church has replaced Israel and that they are God's earthly people with earthly promises and blessings. They vainly imagine that they are advancing God's kingdom on earth.

All dispensationalists understand that there is a difference between Israel and the church of this present age, but the majority of them believe that God set Israel aside when they crucified Christ and that the Body of Christ began on the day of Pentecost in Acts 2. God gave Israel a renewed offer the kingdom in the early Acts period (Lk. 23:34; Acts 3:17-21) and the Body of Christ did not begin until after the fall of Israel and the gospel of the grace of God was revealed to the apostle Paul (1 Tim. 1:15-16; Eph. 3:6; Gal. 1:11-12).

What we believe about when this present dispensation began has major doctrinal and practical ramifications. Most dispensationalists believe that it began at the beginning of Acts in chapter 2 (too early) and a few believe it began at the end in chapter 28 (too late). Acts 2 dispensationalists consider themselves to be "classical dispensationalists" and call our view "hyper-dispensationalism."

Our position is not only attacked by the religious world, but also by some dispensationalists. If you believe the doctrine set forth in this book, you can expect to encounter misrepresentation, straw-man arguments, and slander about your position.

Are we going beyond (i.e., hyper) the word of God to believe that we are to rightly divide the prophetic kingdom program of Israel which concerns that which was spoken by the prophets since the world began (Acts 3:21) from the mystery program of the Body of Christ which concerns that which was kept secret since the world began until it was revealed through the apostle Paul (Rom. 16:25)? Are we going beyond the word of God to believe that Christ chose Paul to be the pattern and spokesman for the Body of Christ to follow in this present dispensation (1 Cor. 4:16-17; 11:1; Phil. 4:9; 1 Tim. 1:12-16)?

This truth is often misunderstood, misrepresented, and just flatly attacked by other professing Christians. Thankfully, there are believers out there who sincerely desire to know the truth of God's word.

The most common attacks against our position are:

1) We make too much of Paul.

We do not exalt Paul as a man or make more out of him than the scripture does; Paul rebuked the carnal Corinthians for that (1 Cor. 1:12-13). It is not the person but the position of Paul that we magnify (Rom. 11:15). We follow Christ in this age by following the pattern and spokesman that He sent to us (Jn. 13:20). Paul wrote the words of Christ (1 Tim. 6:3). By inspiration of God, he told us to follow him and emphasized the importance of his distinct message and ministry. Why doesn't anyone seem to have a problem with the fact that Israel was to follow Moses?

2) We only study Paul's epistles and cannot get a blessing from the rest.

We certainly emphasize Paul's epistles because we know that they were written directly to us in this present age of grace, but we believe, read, and study the whole Bible (2 Tim. 3:16; Rom. 15:4; 1 Cor. 10:11). There are moral principles and spiritual applications for us throughout the scripture. I get more of a blessing from the Old Testament than before I learned how to rightly divide. God said that we are not to add or diminish from His word, which would change it; but He told us to divide His word, which means we get more out of it.

3) Paul said he persecuted the "church of God" before he was saved (1 Cor. 15:9).

What is a church? It is a called-out assembly. We do not read the word church in the Old Testament because it is translated from Greek and not Hebrew. However, we know there was a church in the Old Testament because that is what Stephen said Israel was when they were called out of Egypt and assembled in the wilderness (Acts 7:38). David prophesied of the kingdom church in Psalm 22:22-31. When the writer of Hebrews quoted Psalm 22:22 he said "church" instead of "congregation" (Heb. 2:12). The church in Jerusalem was certainly the church of God, but it was a prophesied church looking for the Messianic kingdom (Acts 1:6; 2:30) and not a mystery hid in God (Eph. 3:9). The Body of Christ is a church, but not every church in the Bible is the Body of Christ. Any church made up of God's people is a church of God. Preachers say, "There is only one church of God," but Paul wrote to "the church of God which at Corinth" and referred to "the churches of God" three times. In the Old Testament we find references to "the congregation of God" and the "congregation of the Lord." Paul said that he "wasted" the church of God (Gal. 1:13). He could do that to a local church, but not to the spiritual Body of Christ.

Another proof text that supposedly refutes our position is Acts 9:4-5, but if you will compare what Christ said concerning how He will judge the nations on the basis of how they treated His brethren (Jews in the tribulation period, Matthew 25:31-46), you will understand that the fact He asked Saul of Tarsus, "Why persecutest thou me?" does not prove he was persecuting the Body of Christ.

4) Paul referred to those who were in Christ before him (Rom. 16:7).

What makes the Body of Christ distinct is not that we are "in Christ," but that we are "one new man" (Eph. 2:15) in which there is neither Jew nor Gentile (Gal. 3:27-28). Every believer that is redeemed by the blood of Christ is "in Christ," and so all believers on this side of the cross are "in Christ." A person can only be "in Adam" or "in Christ" (1 Cor. 15:22). When Israel is saved under the new covenant they will be "in the LORD" but they will still be a distinct nation with authority over the Gentiles (Isa. 45:17; 45:24-25). The tribulation saints that are martyred will "die in the Lord" (Rev. 14:13). In the eternal state, the nation of Israel, the saved Gentile nations, and the Body of Christ will be one family of God, and will all be in Christ, but these groups will remain distinct throughout eternity (Eph. 1:10; 3:14-15).

5) Paul said that he preached the faith he once destroyed (Gal. 1:21-23).

In the context, Paul is defending his distinct apostleship and he makes it clear he was not one of the twelve apostles. He had denied that Jesus was the Christ, the Son of God and persecuted all who believed on Him. Upon his conversion, he began to preach the very faith that he had sought to destroy. However, that was not all he preached for in the context he also speaks of the truth he received by revelation of Jesus Christ (Gal. 1:11-12; 2:1-2).

People also try to use 1 Corinthians 15:11; but the fact that all of the apostles preached the resurrection of Christ does not prove that Paul and the twelve apostles had the same message and ministry. Peter preached that Christ was risen from the dead to sit in the throne of David (Acts 2:30), but Paul preached that Christ was risen from the dead to be the Head of one Body (Eph. 1:20-23; 2 Tim. 2:8).

6) Paul taught that the Body of Christ was formed by the cross (Eph. 2:16).

Notice that he said, "by the cross" and not "at the cross." The cross is the basis upon which God is building the Body of Christ, but it did not mark the historical beginning of it. Not everything Christ accomplished by His cross took effect at the time of His cross (e.g., the destruction of Satan, Rom. 16:20). We become members of the Body of Christ "by one Spirit" (Eph. 2:18) and "by the gospel" (Eph. 3:6). Therefore, how could the Body of Christ begin before the gospel we must believe to be in the Body of Christ was revealed?

7) The Holy Ghost was first poured out on Pentecost.

Christ poured out the Holy Ghost on the Day of Pentecost according to prophecy (Isa. 32:15; Joel 2:28). The Acts 2 dispensationalists make the blunder of thinking that the baptism with the Holy Ghost is the same as the baptism by the Spirit, and they call it the "baptism of the Holy Spirit," a phrase that is not found in the King James Bible. If words have any meaning, they cannot be the same baptism. Christ baptizing saved disciples with the Holy Ghost for power according to prophecy is not the same thing as the Spirit of God baptizing sinners into the Body of Christ for salvation, which was a mystery.

8) Peter preached the cross in the early chapters of Acts.

Of course, Peter preached about the cross in the early chapters of Acts, but how did he preach it? He preached it as a murder indictment on the nation of Israel (Acts 2:36-38; 3:14-15; 4:10; 5:30). He proved that Christ was risen from the dead and that they needed to repent of crucifying Him in order for Him to return and establish His kingdom. Paul was the first one to glory in the cross (Gal. 6:14) and to preach it as good news (1 Cor. 15:3-4).

If you cannot scripturally defend what you believe, you are not rooted and grounded in the truth and are in danger of being "tossed to and fro with every wind of doctrine" (Eph. 4:14).

Chapter 19
The Necessity of Rightly Dividing

Why should we believe so strongly in rightly dividing the word of truth? It is not a novelty (i.e., something new, just to be different), but a biblical necessity. The critics of dispensationalism claim that it was invented by John N. Darby in the 1800's. Actually, it is God's method of Bible study as revealed in His word. In the one verse in which God plainly tells us to study His word, he tells us why and how to do it (2 Tim. 2:15).

All of the Bible is "the word of truth" (Ps. 119:43; 2 Cor. 6:7) and is profitable (2 Tim. 3:16), but there are divisions that God put within His word that we must acknowledge and consistently maintain in our Bible study if we are going to get the profit out of it that He put in it for us.

We must rightly divide the word of truth if we are going to:

1) Present the gospel clearly.

(12) That we should be to the praise of his glory, who first trusted in Christ.
(13) In whom ye also *trusted,* after that ye heard <u>the word of truth, the gospel of your salvation</u>: in whom also after that ye believed, ye were sealed with that holy Spirit of promise, (Eph. 1:12-13)

There is only one gospel by which we can be saved in this present age, but there is certainly more than one gospel in the

Bible. Do you really think that God has given only one message of good news throughout the ages? The gospel of our salvation was revealed by Christ to the apostle Paul (Gal. 1:11-12). The "word of truth" to Israel (Jam. 1:1, 18) is not the word of truth by which we are saved today. This is clearly seen by comparing Acts 2:37-38 with Acts 16:30-31. People will inevitably muddy the waters of the gospel when they fail to rightly divide the word of truth.

2) Understand the Bible.

Consider what I say; and the Lord give thee understanding in all things. (2 Tim. 2:7)

When we understand through Paul's epistles where we are living in God's plan for the ages, the Bible will begin to open more and more to our understanding.

3) Know our identity in Christ.

And ye are complete in him, which is the head of all principality and power: (Col. 2:10)

It is in Paul's epistles alone that we find the heavenly position, conversation, and destiny of the Body of Christ (Eph. 2:6; Phil. 3:20; Col. 3:1-4). We are not Israel, but a new creature (2 Cor. 5:17; Gal. 6:15-16).

4) Know the will of God.
For this cause we also, since the day we heard *it*, do not cease to pray for you, and to desire that ye might be filled

with the knowledge of his will in all wisdom and spiritual understanding; (Col 1:9)

The will of God is revealed in the word of God; and yet most Christians are busy trying to find it in feelings, circumstances, experiences, and religion. The will of God for this present age is revealed in Paul's epistles (Rom. 12:1-2; Eph. 5:14-17). God gives us the liberty to make choices. When we focus on doing the revealed will of God, the details of our life will begin to fall into place (e.g., 1 Tim. 2:4). We must be in line with what God is doing, otherwise, we will experience defeat and discouragement.

5) Live a fruitful Christian life.

That ye might walk worthy of the Lord unto all pleasing, being fruitful in every good work, and increasing in the knowledge of God; (Col 1:10)

Knowing the will of God should lead to doing the will of God. The Christian life will not operate on the basis of ignorance. It is by rightly dividing the word of truth that we learn we are complete in Christ and how to live out that glorious position by faith (Rom. 6:14-17; Col. 2:6-7). The grace life is the Christ life (Gal. 2:20; 4:19; 5:22-23).

6) Look for that blessed hope.

Behold, I shew you a mystery; We shall not all sleep, but we shall all be changed, (1 Cor. 15:51)

Sadly, most professing Christians do not know what the hope of their calling is (Eph. 1:18). They either think Christ is coming to the earth to give them the kingdom (the hope of Israel) or that there will be no kingdom age at all. Many today believe we must go through some or all of the tribulation period. The key to understanding the blessed hope of the Body of Christ is to recognize that it was a mystery revealed to Paul and rightly divide it from Israel's hope. This present age, which was a mystery hid from the prophets, is what is keeping the seventieth week of Daniel from being fulfilled. We are to be looking for Christ from heaven to catch us up to meet Him in the air and give us a glorified body that is fit to reign with Him eternal in the heavens (2 Cor. 5:1; Phil. 3:20-21; Titus 2:13).

7) Be rewarded at the Judgment Seat of Christ.

(10) According to the grace of God which is given unto me, <u>as a wise masterbuilder, I have laid the foundation</u>, and another buildeth thereon. But let every man take heed how he buildeth thereupon.
(11) For other foundation can no man lay than that is laid, which is Jesus Christ.
(12) Now if any man build upon this foundation gold, silver, precious stones, wood, hay, stubble;
(13) Every man's work shall be made manifest: for the day shall declare it, because it shall be revealed by fire; and <u>the fire shall try every man's work of what sort it is</u>.
(14) If any man's work abide which he hath built thereupon, he shall receive a reward.
(15) If any man's work shall be burned, he shall suffer loss: but he himself shall be saved; yet so as by fire.
(1 Cor. 3:10-15)

We will not be "approved" (2 Tim. 2:15) in our service at the Judgment Seat of Christ and receive eternal rewards if we do not follow the example and doctrine of the wise master builder (1 Cor. 4:1-5, 16-17; 11:1; 2 Cor. 5:9-11; 2 Tim. 2:5, 10-13).

As you can see from these seven points, rightly dividing the word of truth is indeed a necessity! All who work to make this truth known can expect satanic opposition. We must depend on God for the strength to keep standing for the word of God rightly divided (Eph. 6:10-20). It is worth it now, but it will especially be worth it in the life to come.

And let us not be weary in well doing: for in due season we shall reap, if we faint not. (Gal 6:9)

Chapter 20
The Fight is On

The theme of Ephesians is the one spiritual church which is the Body of Christ. This great epistle opens with our **spiritual blessings in heavenly places**, and it closes with our **spiritual battle in high places.** Those who will know, believe, and live by the spiritual blessings we have in Christ will quickly become aware of the reality of this great battle.

Outline of Ephesians:
- I.   Introduction (1:1-2)
- II. Edification: Spiritual Wealth (1:3-3:21)
- III. Exhortation: Spiritual Walk (4:1-6:9)
- IV. Enlightenment: Spiritual Warfare (6:10-20)
- V.   Conclusion (6:21-24)

If we are going to serve God, we must fight the good fight of faith as a good soldier of Jesus Christ (1 Tim. 1:18; 6:12; 2 Tim. 2:3). By the way, we are to be "striving together" (Phil. 1:27) and not striving against one another. Satan will constantly attack the unity of any assembly that stands for the truth of the one Body of Christ (Eph. 4:1-6).

We are not fighting against flesh and blood enemies. Satan certainly uses men (Eph. 4:14), but we must see beyond the people he uses and understand what he is doing in opposition to God's purpose and plan.

There is a vast spirit world that is invisible (Col. 1:16) to our physical eyes, but we can know the truth about it from the word of God. The principalities (territories of a prince), powers (authorities), and rulers (princes) that we fight against have to do with spiritual wickedness in high places (Eph. 6:12).

Satan always opposes what God is doing, and how he works is always in accordance with how God is working. The most important thing is to know who God is and what He is doing, but after that you had better learn about who the devil is and what he is doing in opposition to God's work. God changes in His dealings with men throughout the ages, and so does Satan.

When Christ was on the earth doing visible signs and wonders, Satan's opposition was also visible. God is working spiritually, not visibly, in this present age. Therefore, Satan is also working spiritually and not visibly. Paul warns us again and again about spiritual deception (e.g., 1 Tim. 4:1; 2 Tim. 3:13). If we fail to put on the whole armor of God, we will not be able to stand against the wiles of the devil.

What is God's will in this present age (1 Tim. 2:4; Col. 1:23-29)?
- all men to be saved = the gospel of the grace of God
- and to come unto the knowledge of the truth = the mystery of the Body of Christ

Therefore, Satan is working to (2 Cor. 4:3-4; 11:3):
- blind sinners to the gospel = with counterfeit gospels
- blind saints to the mystery = with religious traditions

Satan's mystery of iniquity which has to do with religion (2 Thess. 2:7; 2 Tim. 3:5) works in opposition to God's mystery of godliness which is the Body of Christ (1 Tim. 3:14-16).

A Parallel

Israel is God's earthly people: a physical nation given a literal land on the earth. God gave Israel a piece of land, and they had to fight flesh and blood enemies to possess and enjoy what was already theirs. The Body of Christ is His heavenly people (Eph. 2:6). God has given us "all spiritual blessings in heavenly places," and we must fight spiritual enemies to appropriate and enjoy what is already ours. Just as Israel was to fight their enemies by depending on the power of God, we must be "strong in the Lord, and in the power of His might" if we are going to stand against our enemies.

In the book of Exodus, God redeemed Israel out of Egypt. In the book of Joshua, He brought them into the land of promise. In between those books, in the book of Numbers, we see that Israel failed to possess their land at the first because of unbelief and therefore they wandered in the wilderness.

The book of Romans (our Exodus) teaches us about our redemption by the blood of Christ. The book of Ephesians (our Joshua) teaches us about the spiritual blessings God wants us to walk in and enjoy. In between those books, in 1 Corinthians and Galatians (our Numbers), we learn that it is possible for believers to not appropriate who they are in Christ because of unbelief, and therefore wander in a spiritual wilderness.

Like the children of Israel in Kadesh Barnea, there are professing Christians today who will come right up to the border of understanding the word of God rightly divided and what it means to be God's heavenly people but turn back for fear of the opposition that awaits them.

We cannot prevail against Satan in our own strength. We have the victory in Christ. He has furnished us with the armor we need to war a good warfare.

Paul liked to use metaphors, and he was certainly familiar with the armor of a Roman soldier, as he was probably being guarded by one as he wrote this epistle. In this passage he uses the pieces of the soldier's armor metaphorically to teach about the spiritual qualities we must walk in each day if we are going to stand in the evil day. The picture is that of a soldier fully dressed in armor and standing ready to fight.

(10) Finally, my brethren, be strong in the Lord, and in the power of his might.
(11) Put on the whole armour of God, that ye may be able to stand against the wiles of the devil.
(12) For we wrestle not against flesh and blood, but against principalities, against powers, against the rulers of the darkness of this world, against spiritual wickedness in high places.
(13) Wherefore take unto you the whole armour of God, that ye may be able to withstand in the evil day, and having done all, to stand.
(14) Stand therefore, having your loins girt about with truth, and having on the breastplate of righteousness;

(15) And your feet shod with the preparation of the gospel of peace;
(16) Above all, taking the shield of faith, wherewith ye shall be able to quench all the fiery darts of the wicked.
(17) And take the helmet of salvation, and the sword of the Spirit, which is the word of God:
(18) Praying always with all prayer and supplication in the Spirit, and watching thereunto with all perseverance and supplication for all saints;
(19) And for me, that utterance may be given unto me, that I may open my mouth boldly, to make known the mystery of the gospel,
(20) For which I am an ambassador in bonds: that therein I may speak boldly, as I ought to speak. (Eph. 6:10-20)

Consider some highlights from this great passage.

- Notice how Paul called it the WHOLE armor of God. He mentions seven pieces (the number of perfection). If we leave off a piece, Satan will find that opening.
- It is God's responsibility to provide the armor, but it is our responsibility to put it on.
- A spiritual war against spiritual enemies requires spiritual weapons (2 Cor. 10:3-6). The Bible is our main offensive weapon. With this sharp sword we may cut spiritual enemies (Heb. 4:12). That God promised to provide us with the sword of the Spirit proves that we still have the inspired word of God today. Satan hates the word of God and has attacked it from the beginning (Gen. 3:1). He wants to replace our sharp sword with something else. Most professing Christians today are using a butter knife in the form of corrupt modern versions, instead of a two-

edged sword, the pure King James Bible. Among those that use the sword of the Spirit, many do not know how to handle it (Heb. 5:11-14; 2 Tim. 2:15). With the sword of the Spirit, we may: defeat temptation (Matt. 4:1-11; 1 Cor. 10:13), evangelize the lost, and build believers up in the faith.

- To put on this spiritual armor is to put on Christ (Rom. 13:11-14). We must have the armor of light to fight against spiritual darkness. As to our standing, we put on Christ the moment of salvation. But as to our state, we must put on Christ by faith in our daily walk.
- Every piece is connected to the word of God. The central piece is the shield of faith because it is believing the word that activates the armor (Prov. 30:5-6).

We should desire to reach as many people as possible. Sadly, it seems that less and less people are interested in the truth of God's word rightly divided. In this evil day, we must STAND (Eph. 6:11, 13-14). It is our responsibility to share the truth, but we cannot make anybody receive it. Regardless of how people respond, it glorifies God when we work to make His truth known to others (2 Tim. 4:1-5).

Therefore, my beloved brethren, be ye stedfast, unmoveable, always abounding in the work of the Lord, forasmuch as ye know that your labour is not in vain in the Lord. (1 Cor. 15:58)

Other Books by David O'Steen

Study Notes on Basic Bible Truth
Study Notes on the King James Bible
Study Notes on Books of the Bible
Study Notes on the Book of Acts
Study Notes on Colossians
Study Notes on the Epistles of Peter

Links to purchase the Study Notes books are found on our church website (click on Books under Resources).

For hundreds of Bible studies and messages in audio, video, and written format, please visit:

www.hopebiblechurchga.com

Hope Bible Church
199 Four Points Rd.
Jackson, GA 30233

Printed in Dunstable, United Kingdom